Old Forms On a New Land

EUREKA.

Samuel & Jos. C. Newsom
Architects
504 Kearny St
Top Floor
San Francisco.
Cal.

Scale   Feet

FRONT ELEVATION

Old Forms On a New Land

CALIFORNIA ARCHITECTURE IN PERSPECTIVE

Harold Kirker

ROBERTS RINEHART PUBLISHERS
An Arpel Graphics Book

Published by Roberts Rinehart Publishers
Post Office Box 666, Niwot, Colorado 80544
International Standard Book Number 0-911797-89-0
Library of Congress Catalog Card Number 91-60851
Printed in the United States of America

To James Kirker

Contents

Illustrations

Acknowledgments

From the Yurok Indians to the Post-Modernists, Californians have imposed inherited building forms upon a land whose extraordinary diversity has encouraged every kind of colonialism. The architectural traditions of Siberia, the Mediterranean, North Europe, and all the regions of the United States, as well as every stylistic revival of the last century and a half, have been transplanted in California. This book tells the story of their origins, domestication, and adaptation.

Among many who contributed to the making of this book, I wish to thank particularly David Gebhard of the University of California, Santa Barbara, for critically reading the manuscript; James D. Hart and his associates at the Bancroft Library of the University of California, Berkeley, for advice and assistance over many years; Thomas S. Hines of the University of California, Los Angeles, for steadfast encouragement and friendship; and Norris Hundley of the University of California, Los Angeles, for cheerful, sensitive, and sustained editorial guidance.

Harold Kirker
Santa Barbara
1991

1. Mattz House, Crescent City, ca. 1850. Courtesy of the National Geographic Society, *World of the American Indian,* 1974, page 246. Photographer David Hiser.

I

Indian Builders

The precise origins of the first Californians are conjectural. However, the theory that many of them emigrated from northeastern Asia in the last ice age by means of a land bridge over what is now the Bering Strait seems to be supported by the Siberian building culture of the Yuroks. Similarities between the subterranean lodges of the Miwoks and Pomos and those of the Southwest and northern Mexico also suggest that some native peoples drifted southeastward in a great evolutionary circle that probably also had its beginnings in Beringia.

Amid these speculations is the certainty that the first Californians composed the largest regional Indian body in what is presently the continental United States: about 300,000 or perhaps a fifth of the total native population at the time of Spanish colonization. The motivation for the successive Stone Age migrations was apparently the chase, and the California Indians remained hunters and gatherers down to the time of their near extinction at the end of the nineteenth century. Although they raised few crops, kept no herds, and had neither the wheel nor the plow, the culture they brought with them was not only sufficient for their needs but probably far richer than present evidence suggests. The land, which must have seemed as benign and bountiful to these first colonists as it had to the subsequent waves of immigrants whose activities constitute the state's recorded history, provided an abundance of game, acorns, and grass; the sea, lakes, and rivers also gave generously from their store. The exploitation of these natural food sources resulted in the production of watertight baskets and skillfully joined canoes that could carry a dozen men upon the open sea. These artifacts have been judged the finest of their kind among the Indians of North America, and while no comparable architectural evidence has survived, these same skills, refined and redirected by Franciscan missionaries in the late eighteenth and early nineteenth centuries, contributed substantially to the architecture that constitutes Hispanic California's finest material heritage.

The benevolent circumstances that restrained agricultural development also determined California's earliest habitations. After food itself, shelter undoubtedly reflected more faithfully than any other element the comfortable relationship that existed between the Indians and the land. Contemporary accounts of pre-Franciscan building are confined largely to the Chumash of the Santa Barbara Channel, whose huts of brush and earth were often and favorably remarked upon by the early Spanish diarists. Some described these dwellings as shaped like cones; others as resembling a half-cut orange. All agreed that they were neatly constructed by placing slender poles in a circle and drawing them together at the top to form a frame over which was laid earth, branches, brush, tule mats, or thatch woven from sea grass. In the construction of the typical willow frame, earthen walls could be raised only to a height of several feet from the ground; where heavier wood, such as pine or oak, was used, dirt was plastered over the entire surface to form a wattle-like covering. Generally there were two entrances and a smoke hole was punched through the frame at the center; the door was a mat that swung inward like a screen and was secured by whalebone or stick.[1]

Like all California dwellings prior to the development of an American building style at Monterey after 1835, the Chumash houses contained little furniture other than raised beds spread with sleeping mats of woven reeds. Designed as temporary shelters to accommodate four or five families, they were periodically replaced by burning. With a few notable exceptions, such as the wooden houses of the Yuroks in the extreme northwest, the hemispherical shelter of the Chumash can serve as the prototype California Indian dwelling. It was simply constructed of materials, which although varying from region to region, were always at hand and easily and quickly worked. And whether seaweed-thatched, mud-plastered, or skin-covered, the structure was adequate to the needs of people who had few possessions and lived most of their lives outdoors in a temperate climate.

In extreme northwestern California, where the weather is less favorable, the Yurok Indians followed a building practice of probable Siberian derivation. A rare extant example of their craft, said to date from about mid-nineteenth century, appears in the Mattz House, shown in Plate 1. The close and striking relationship between this structure and those which survive along the North Pacific Coast, and the earlier but lost Russian architecture at Fort Ross, sustains the belief that north European building traditions first reached California via Siberia, Alaska, and Beringia. The Mattz House is a fairly accurate example of the fitted-frame Yurok dwelling constructed—without post or beam—of split or hewn planks of uneven length set endwise in the ground and lashed through holes to exterior and interior horizontal poles; the whole of which is enclosed by a subterranean chamber generally fourteen feet in diameter and four in depth. Building types varied somewhat among the Indians of the northwestern counties, and that represented in the Mattz House, like most survivors from the past, is not only a superior example but represents accretions from later times.

The Mattz House does not have the usual ragged appearance of traditional Yurok dwellings, particularly the jagged eaves that resulted from a technology without axe or saw. The roof rigging is obviously not authentic; Indians used grape vines or hazel twigs and not rope in pre-Hispanic construction. The Mattz House is typical, however, in having two ridges and three roof slopes, the consequence of the general practice of making side walls lower than those in front and rear. Traditional also is the door plank carved in geometric relief. Clearly visible in Plate 1 is the pair of gripstones invariably placed at the entrance to ease the householder's exit through the low doorway from the shelf that surrounded the excavated core of the shelter; a similar set of stones was set just inside the doorway to assist entry into the dwelling. The opening was closed by a fitted panel and the element of comfort, so important in the life of the Yuroks, was heightened by a fire burning continually in the center of the recessed floor. A smoke hole, serving also as a window, was made by pushing aside a board in the middle of the roof. In rainy weather this was raised up by a stick to form a protective lean-to; a line of gutters gouged out of the sides of the smoke hole prevented water from flowing into the snug interior. In contrast to the expendable character of the usual California Indian brush, earthen, or skin shelters, the Yurok dwellings were permanent homes, thoughtfully fitted into a natural slope or a grove of trees and each given an individual and identifying name.[2]

With the significant exception of the Colorado River tribes, the first known Californians shared in common only one building form other than shelter: the *temescal* or sweat house. The primary purpose of the sweat house seems to have been more religious than therapeutic, although it had important medicinal properties as well as serving as a club or assembly place for men. Women did not share in the latter functions, but they were admitted on ceremonial occasion. Traditionally the sweat house was subterranean or at least partially dug out. The variations in the superstructure reflected regional characteristics: with the dome builders it was hemispherical and roofed with earth, tule, or animal skins and the excavation was shallow; the wood workers of the Northwest erected a fitted frame that enclosed a large dugout at least four feet deep. In every case, construction was substantial in order to retain the heat, which was generated directly by fire and not steam. The entrance was in the middle of the structure, facing ocean, river, or lake, in which the participants immersed themselves after sweating. There was little, if any, furnishing in the sweat house; the exception being the comfort-prone Yuroks who introduced redwood-block pillows and erected a sacred pole opposite the fire—whose wood was gathered in accordance with ritualistic formula. The Yuroks paved the interiors of their sweat houses with matched stones or carefully adzed planks. Equally sophisticated was their habit of laying out a stone terrace on the front, where the elder tribesmen sunned themselves and gathered for social intercourse. The considerable attention generally given to the construction of sweat houses and the care usually lavished upon their maintenance supports the belief that this was the most important Native American institution in California.[3]

The knowledge of California architecture prior to Spanish colonization is derived from eighteenth-century descriptions of the Chumash shelters and revealed by the framed houses and *temescals* of the Yuroks that survived long enough to be scientifically studied and documented. The latter furnish an essential element in a material culture characterized by the anthropologist A. L. Kroeber as "un-Californian." For the Yurok structures, common to the Pacific Coast and northwestern California, represented a building tradition that was brought from northeastern Asia millennia ago and practiced in the new world without important deviation. This does not mean that the Yuroks were innately incapable of change or invention. They shared, for example, in what has been called one of early California's greatest achievements: the development of a leaching process by which acorns were rendered into nutritious food by the removal of tannic acid. The perfecting of this technology fostered, in turn, the production of water-tight baskets for which the California Indians, and particularly the Yuroks, are famous. In matters of shelter, however, there was no necessity to invent new forms or depart from long-established practices. The ancient wood tradition brought by the Yuroks was easily, and appropriately, transplanted to the cool, damp forests of northern California. Their buildings, far more structurally complex than the simpler shelters of the Chumash, represent a notable early example of the architectural colonialism that was repeated by every successive immigrant group. The diversity of California's natural environment, which somewhere offers almost every physical feature of the earth, encourages accommodation and discourages innovation. Freed from the necessity to alter basic inherited forms and make them conform to radically different natural conditions, the earliest Californians to leave a tangible record on the land, like the latest, utilized the building tradition they brought with them.

2. Mission Santa Barbara, 1815–1820. Courtesy of the Santa Barbara Historical Society.

II

Hispanic Builders

The Hispanic civilization of Alta California was characterized by lateness in time, briefness in duration, and neglectfulness in administration. Although first explored by Juan Rodriquez Cabrillo in the mid-sixteenth century, California was disregarded for over two hundred years by a succession of Spanish authorities who considered its coastal area merely an isolated and dangerous passage for the single Manila Galleon annually bound for Acapulco. It was only when this exposed area appeared threatened from the north that a belated settlement by Gaspar de Portolá was undertaken in 1769 with the principal motive of defense joined to traditional religious objectives.

Not organized for colonization in the Anglo-American sense, Portolá's mission to California was designed mainly to forestall England's drive across Canada and down the Pacific Coast; a secondary consideration was the containment of Russia's southward advance from the recently discovered Aleutian Islands. Yet even this slender foothold was grudgingly sustained. Portolá himself declared that Spain did not want California and warned that its defense would require the expenditure of hugh sums of money and the sacrifice of thousands of lives. Portolá's conclusion was based on the extreme geographic isolation of California, a condition that continued to determine the life of the land until the coming of the railroad in 1869. In the Spanish period, moreover, California's natural isolation was reinforced by attempts to impose a central economic policy that prohibited foreign trade. This policy continued officially until Mexican independence was declared in California in 1822, when its repudiation encouraged an influx of foreign traders. The new government's secularization of the vast mission lands and the corresponding rise of the rancho—which resulted in the nearly complete disintegration of Indian life—created a valuable trade in hides that was rapidly absorbed by the foreigners. These merchants and adventurers, of whom the majority were American, assumed an economic and cultural dominance during the troubled period of nominal Mexican rule that led to an American conquest in 1846. Long before that time, however, California had become an architectural colony of the United States.

The Hispanic architecture of California was preeminently the art of the mission builders. The structures these Franciscan builders laid upon the land, which remain as the enduring material complement to their spiritual mission, are California's finest colonial monuments. But in the initial stage of colonization, the temporary structures erected by the Spanish settlers were hardly distinguishable from those of the Chumash prototype. The indigenous brush hut, however, was soon replaced by the *palizada* lodge, the Spanish variant of the log house or stockade. This typical frontier structure was erected of pine or cypress poles set upright in the ground and bound together by reeds or leather thongs. Plastered inside and out with clay and heavily whitewashed with lime made from sea shells, the palisade lodge was roofed with poles over which branches were laid and the whole covered with earth. The colonists also adopted the Indian method of thatching with tule, and, despite its flammable quality, the tule roof was used almost exclusively in secular construction until at least the Mexican period, when Spanish tile and eventually American wood shakes and shingles replaced thatch in domestic buildings.

The scarcity of wood in the vicinity of the few isolated outposts planted along the coast merely reinforced the colonists' historic Mediterranean masonry tradition, and adobe brick remained the most easily attainable building material in the Hispanic period. The various methods used to compensate for the low-bearing capacity of adobe, as well as its extreme susceptibility to weather and water erosion, resulted in thick walls repeatedly plastered and broken only infrequently by door and window openings. Despite legend, the sheltering *corridor* was not an invariable component of the primitive building culture of presido and pueblo; its employment, like the early use of tile, was limited largely to mission construction. The Franciscans, unlike their contemporary lay builders, used stone or kiln-burned brick whenever possible, as opposed to sun-dried adobe. Where necessity required adobe, the mission builders faced it with brick masonry and spanned the openings with brick arches or wooden lintels. It was the Franciscans, working with more durable materials and wider cultural traditions, who produced the

8   OLD FORMS ON A NEW LAND

familiar and romantic mission forms that legend has invested in the secular architecture of Spanish California.

The colonial builders of California were aided in conserving established methods of construction and patterns of style by the extraordinary diversity of the land. The suitability with which the earlier Siberian emigrants established their historic wood tradition in the cool, damp forests of northern California had its parallel in the transplanting of inherited building forms by the Hispanic settlers on the coastal plains of southern California with their familiar lack of wood, water, and shade. The latter's Mediterranean building tradition was a Mexican variant of an architectural legacy left to Spain by successive Roman and Moorish colonists. In fact, it can be said that Spain's architecture reached California at least third hand, having undergone many New World adaptations by the time of Portolá's initial settlement in 1769. This contrasts with the example of some of the later American colonies, particularly those of the English, who implemented an architectural tradition that came directly from the homeland via the Atlantic passage.

However, in all cases, it is impossible to understand the building practices of North America's colonists without reference to the principal institutions of their European sources. Spain had an autocratic government, a unified church, and an overseas economy based largely on colonialism. The institutions of state and church were joined by common, and fervent, objectives to which the colonies were subject. The two ruling hierarchies also shared a variegated architecture— evolved from Roman aqueducts, Moorish mosques, Romanesque monasteries, Gothic cathedrals, and Renaissance palaces—in which the functions of state and church were often indistinguishable. The Spanish colonists thus coupled a particular national spirit concentrated in the preservation of religious orthodoxy with the general inclination to preserve building traditions. Yet in the extension of their old building forms on the new land, there were inevitable deviations from the mother country necessitated by regional conditions and unavoidable cultural borrowings. This was especially true in California, where settlement occurred only half a century before the disintegration of the Spanish colonial empire in America.

In this climate of weakness and decline, the national building forms, which had already undergone modification in Mexico, were further simplified in California. An important factor in this simplifying process was the lack of immigrant craftsmen and the relatively primitive state of Indian building skills as compared to those of the Mayan and Aztec inheritors. As can be seen in Plate 2, these limitations gave the California mission its characteristic structural frankness; a quality conveyed by broad, largely unrelieved walls, massive arcades, and low, sheltering roofs of heavy tile. The effect is of primitive and powerful force; the manifestation in a remote colony of the impassioned central goal of the motherland. The substitution at Santa Barbara of square piers for the traditional colonnade of the cloisters of Spain and Mexico suggests modifications necessitated by the scarcity of trained labor. Yet in comparison to most California missions, the mission at Santa Barbara is exceptional, owing its origin to a plate in an eighteenth-century Spanish edition of Vitruvius carried into the wilderness by Father Antonio Ripoll, who reconstructed the church after the disastrous earthquake of 1812.

The extremely lavish ornamentation that enriched the facades of the great Mexican versions of Spanish churches was scarcely considered in California. When attempts were made to apply even the most restrained decoration, as at San Diego de Alcalá, they emerged as ghostly suggestions around key openings in massive blank walls. The traditional Spanish *campanario,* or pierced belfrey, was generally modified in California to a simple wall in which bells were hung in modest sequence, as at Santa Inez, or with forceful assymmetry as at San Gabriel Arcángel. An example of how Spanish influence occasionally reached California directly is the south facade of San Gabriel, where the capped buttresses and tall narrow windows replicate the cathedral at Cordova (formerly a mosque), in which the mission's builder Antonio Cruzado was trained before going to Mexico. But these references could have reached California just as easily via the more usual Mexican route. Father Cruzado, like most of his Francisca brethren, was familiar with the great sixteenth-century fortress-missions in the Valley of Mexico, whose heavy, crowned buttresses recalled the Moorish architectural heritage of Old Spain.

The architecture of the Franciscan missions conveys the colonial character acquired in America by an institution whose purpose originated in Spain and underwent centuries of New World testing prior to establishment in California. The mission system was designed to foster in the wilderness a Christian conversion that would equip the Indian neophyte for citizenship within the institutions of a self-sufficient community. The degree to which these objectives were achieved, and at what cost, is the subject of continuing controversy. However, judging from architectural evidence alone, the missionary effort in California was successful. The Franciscans understood that in the absence of appreciable numbers of Hispanic-emigrant craftsmen, the projected missions could be constructed only by Indians trained in new skills within a single generation. In 1776, ten years before the founding of Mission Santa Barbara, Father Pedro Font described the Channel Island Indians as "so ingenious and so industrious [that they] would become experts if they had teachers and suitable tools."[1]

The chief instructors of the neophytes were the Franciscans, who were occasionally aided by itinerant Americans such as Thomas Doak, who painted the reredos in Mission San Juan Bautista. However, they relied largely upon the assistance of a small group of skilled craftsmen-teachers from Baja California: masons, carpenters, and blacksmiths who themselves were generally mission-trained Indians. The learning process was eased by the fact that early Franciscan building embodied such traditional Indian elements as willow-pole construction and tule thatching. Before permanent building could commence, however, the neophytes had to learn to fell trees and shape beams, prepare masonry foundations, make and lay adobe bricks, construct roof and floor tiles, and decorate interior church walls and ceilings. The architectural results of this collaboration, although evident to some degree in each of the twenty-one missions that stretch in a 650-mile chain from San Diego north to Sonoma, can best be read at Santa Barbara, whose mission church survives essentially as constructed (Plate 2). This is the single mission to remain continually under Franciscan care and one of only several to escape the ruin that followed the Mexican decree of secularization in 1833.

The secularization order resulted in the confiscation of the mission lands, the pillage of the mission buildings, and the forced abandonment of the neophytes to death or rancho peonage. The newly-learned Indian skills were generally unused, and, with several notable exceptions, the Franciscan establishments were reduced to picturesque ruin. They remained in a state of isolation and neglect until the last decades of the nineteenth century, when they were discovered as a regional source for a romantic revival. Subsequently restored with varying degrees of authenticity, the missions survive as the preeminent architectural expression of California's colonial past.

The commanding place held by the mission in Hispanic California indicates its institutional significance. For despite the original intent of Spanish colonization, neither presidio nor pueblo acquired the mission's material and historical importance. Instead of affording military protection against foreign encroachment, the helplessness of the presidios invited invasion. Monterey, the capital of California and its major presidio under both Spanish and Mexican rule, was described by Captain George Vancouver two decades after its founding in 1770

3. Casa de Soto, Monterey, ca. 1820. Donald R. Hannaford and Revel Edwards, *Spanish Colonial or Adobe Architecture of California, 1800–1850* (New York: Architectural Book Publishing Company, 1931), p. 61.

as "wretched" and "defenseless"; it was sacked after feeble resistence by Hippolyte de Bouchard under Argentinian flag in 1818, and less than thirty years later was taken by United States naval forces without the firing of a shot. Long before that event, however, the neighboring northern pueblo of Branciforte simply vanished along with its five settlers and seven tule-thatched huts.

The architectural evidence records the relative material insignificance of presidio and pueblo. "The houses here," wrote Richard Henry Dana of Monterey in 1835, "as everywhere in California, are of one story, built of adobe. . . . The floors are generally of earth, the windows grated and without glass."[2] Dana noted further that they were without entries, halls, chimneys, or fireplaces, and their furniture was as simple as their architecture. The Casa de Soto (Plate 3) faithfully confirms Dana's classic description of secular building in the colonial period. As originally constructed by Joaquin de Sota in the last years of Spanish rule, the adobe was roofed with tule; at a later date it was covered with Indian-made tile, probably removed from nearby Mission San Carlos Borromeo. The adobe bricks, until recently exposed as shown in Plate 3, are one and one-half feet square, three feet thick, and bound together with a mixture of mud, broken tile, and twigs. This typical adobe structure accurately expresses the isolation of the Hispanic settlements, their lack of professional building skills, and the subsistence level of a society that had no need for civic or commercial construction.

In its similarity to the Mexican dwellings of the period, the Casa de Soto shows both the social and economic order and the cultural conservatism of the Hispanic colonists in California, who built houses as nearly alike as possible to the ones they left behind. Primitive though it was—lacking every amenity legend has endowed the California provincial house—the Casa de Soto records a simple, open, and generous life lived as much as possible out of doors. Because of this, and despite a recent historically inaccurate restoration, the de Soto adobe furnishes perhaps the finest extant artifactual evidence of the state of building prior to the Yankee milling operations that radically altered the character of domestic architecture in California and created its first modern style.

4. Larkin House, Monterey, 1835–1837. Photograph by Greg Alcorn.

III

American Architectural Conquest

At the same time Richard Henry Dana described the dwellings of Monterey as adobe cottages roofed with thatch and tile, his fellow New Englanders, Thomas Oliver Larkin and Alpheus P. Thompson, were building two-story, adobe-walled houses with joists, rafters, floors, and roofs of milled lumber that would provide one of the earliest physical indication of the province's American destiny (Plate 4).[1] This pioneering building has been labeled the Monterey Style, deriving its name from the colonial capital in California. Historically, it pertains to the decade immediately preceding the American takeover in 1846, and testifies to a significant but brief cultural compromise between the materially weak Hispanic population and an increasingly influential Yankee minority. In combining Spanish masonry and American wood building traditions, Larkin and other Anglo and Hispanic builders gave California its first important domestic vernacular. More significantly, these architectural innovators imposed upon almost every inhabited part of the province visual evidence of the comfort and convenience that accompanied Yankee ingenuity and hegemony. The Monterey Style house was more than the physical setting for the dominant commercial and ranching life of provincial California; it contained, in the minds of leading *Californios*, a promise of the future open to the province should it consent to American annexation.

The architectural conquest of California was preceded by more than a decade of vigorous American economic penetration. As early as 1796, tenuous United States contact with California began when the Boston ship *Otter,* bound for Canton and in desperate need, was admitted in a friendly fashion to the port of Monterey by Governor Diego de Borica. Two years later, agents for the Boston firm of James and Thomas H. Perkins established a pattern of illicit transactions with California ports known locally as the "China trade." Under the pretext of emergency relief, and with the connivance of Spanish authorities, a clandestine exchange of otter skins for such American products as gun powder, blue cloth, dishes, knives, and handsaws was carried out in some secluded cove or offshore island. In the absence of regular supply vessels from Mexico, this contraband traffic was tolerated by local authorities as the only means by which the Spanish colony could maintain more than a minimal subsistence level. With the advent of Mexican rule, American trade was openly promoted. The classic statement of this trade was given by Richard Henry Dana in his literary chronicle of Hispanic California as consisting "of everything under the sun," and its all-encompassing nature was an essential step in the process that gradually transformed the living conditions of Hispanic California.

Thomas Larkin, the province's principal merchant, began building his house in April 1835, after his marriage to Rachel Hobson Holmes of Massachusetts—the first woman of United States nationality to live in California. The house took several years to complete at a cost reckoned to be five thousand dollars.[2] The builder's meticulously kept account books make it possible to follow construction from day to day and show that building an American house in colonial California was an arduous and uncertain undertaking. The basic problem was the lack of an organized building profession and the necessity to import almost every item used in construction other than lumber and adobe. Glass, lead, paint, hardware, wallpaper, and household furnishings were shipped from Boston at high prices and with indeterminate delivery. The woodwork on the house, both structural and cabinet making, was done largely by former ship's carpenters. These wood-workers were often deserters from merchantmen and whalers who accepted employment as foremen among the Mexican laborers hired by Larkin to fell the Santa Cruz redwoods. Larkin's crews converted the redwoods to heavy timber and boards—first for the Hawaiian trade and then, particularly after 1840, for the domestic architectural construction. In the early operations primitive tools, such as whipsaw and adze, were used; subsequently a small mill was imported from Boston and mechanization gradually took over.

Larkin's house was very expensive for the period and testifies to the extraordinary business success achieved by its builder during a California residence of

OLD FORMS ON A NEW LAND

less than five years. The largest single item was the roof, which required 21,000 shingles and cost $581, including $3 for "Rum for Raising the roof." If, contrary to legend, this was not the first shingle roof in Calfornia, it was the most impressive to date. Also impressive was the interior of the Larkin House, which introduced into Hispanic building such standard American features as interior wallpapering, milled doors, and double-hung sash windows. It is believed that as originally constructed, the first floor was divided into a store and storeroom, with a central staircase mounting to the second floor, in which were located the family living quarters. Here was placed the furniture known through the account books to have been imported from Boston: sofas, sideboards, tables, chairs, bedsteads, mirrors, desks. Such unprecedented furnishings not only set an example shortly thereafter emulated by the prominent Hispanic families, but was essential to the lavish entertainment incumbent upon Larkin as the first (and last) United States consul in California. Some of this furniture is reputed to have been returned from Mrs. Toulmin's former home, when the house was purchased in 1922 by Alice Larkin Toulmin, the builder's granddaughter, and remained in it when the historic adobe was deeded to the state of California in 1957 as a monument to Monterey's colonial architecture.

Larkin built, as much as possible, from the memory of buildings he knew in Massachusetts and the Carolinas. He had to accept adobe wall construction and hence deepened the eaves on one front, scaffolded another, and added the double veranda that became one of the distinctive features of the Monterey Style. The presence of a double veranda on a New Englander's house has been the subject of some conjecture. So far as is known, this particular form was introduced into the environs of Boston in the early nineteenth century, presumably from the South. The origin of the two-story veranda can be found in both French Colonial architecture of the Mississippi Valley—the most famous extant example is Connelly's Tavern in Natchez, Mississippi (c. 1796)—and the British West Indies, from which the veranda was introduced into South Carolina in the early eighteenth century. Larkin, who lived in North Carolina between 1821 and 1831, makes diary mention of "piazzas" in at least two entries, and he correctly ascribes this feature in regional architecture to South Carolinian origin.

Foreign trade created the town of Monterey, and in the building which this trade induced can be read its origin and influences. It is estimated that in 1841 New England accounted for eighty percent of Monterey's foreign imports and only slightly less of her exports. Historically, Boston ideas accompanied Boston goods.

Architecture followed the flag; the historic building forms of the eastern seaboard, especially of maritime Massachusetts, helped fill the material void of Arcadian California. But it took time and the application of technology before houses such as Larkin's could be replicated from Los Angeles to Sonoma by a host of ambitious and interrelated Yankee and Mexican families. In 1840, however, Larkin began the first large scale milling operations in the province in the Santa Cruz redwood groves. By his own reckoning there were then in the vicinity of Monterey nearly fifty Anglo-Americans with professions associated with or useful to the building trades. These men, with the aid of imported milling equipment, supplied the skill and muscle for California's first building boom.

In spreading the Monterey building style throughout Mexican-occupied California in the decade between construction of the Larkin House and annexation, the role of family relationships appears to have been crucial. In 1846 Lieutenant Joseph Warren Revere, an American naval officer in Monterey, noted: "The Californians are nearly all related or connected in one way or another. . . . The clanship of Scotland, and the cousinship of New England, are not more remarkable than the kinship of California."[3] The key to this kinship, in so far as it affected regional architecture, was probably General Mariano Guadalupe Vallejo, who was connected with almost every Monterey Style builder as well as being himself the most enthusiastic exponent of the style. Larkin, through his half-brother, John Rogers Cooper, was brother-in-law to the general's sister, Encarnación. Another sister, Rosalia (Señora Jacob C. Leese), became the second mistress of the Larkin House when her American-born husband acquired the property in 1849. The much restored Casa Amesti in Monterey was built for a third sister, Prudenciana, and it was she who transformed it into something resembling its present form. Governor Juan Bautista Alvarado, builder of what is thought to be the provincial capital's second Monterey Style house was Vallejo's nephew—although they were of the same age.

Through both his mother and his wife, General Vallejo was connected with the Carrillo family of San Diego and Santa Barbara, whose most notable member, Carlos Antonio Carrillo, had five daughters married to Americans. Among these were Alpheus B. Thompson of Maine, who built, in Santa Barbara, an important house in the Monterey tradition, and the Bostonian William Goodwin Dana, cousin of Richard Henry Dana and builder of a surviving house at Nipomo in San Luis Obispo County that was noted for its Yankee character. Dana is one of only several men designated as "architect" in the annals of provincial California.[4] Other

18   OLD FORMS ON A NEW LAND

representative Monterey Style houses were built by family relations as far south as Los Angeles, where a fine dwelling was erected in 1841 for Vallejo's uncle, Vincente Lugo. Vallejo was also related to the Castros, some of whose Monterey Style houses are preserved in San Juan Bautista and in the San Francisco Bay Area. Even further north, at the extreme limits of the Mexican province, General Vallejo and his brother Salvador, and their brothers-in-law Jacob Leese and Henry Delano Fitch, all built American houses at Sonoma for their *Californio* wives. The zeal and speed with which the prominent Hispanic families either built or rebuilt in the Monterey Tradition expressed their dissatisfaction with the state of native building technology as well as their acceptance of American material civilization.

The principal extant Monterey Style houses, such as those of Thomas Larkin and the far more massive manorhouse-fortress completed in 1841 by General Vallejo on his Petaluma ranch, are rare artifactual evidence of a period in California's history known chiefly through legend. This brief interval between Spanish and American rule concerned an isolated and rudimental society whose leaders were a small number of foreign merchants and ranchers and the Hispanic families among whom they traded, married, and built. It is this society—nostalgically primitive compared to its successor—that is exemplified in the Monterey Style of architecture. Emanating principally from the provincial capital and Santa Barbara, the style was copied throughout the geographically large but sparsely settled province of California. Its wide acceptance within a few years over the four-hundred mile stretch between San Pedro and Sonoma, records the growing power of Anglo traditions over the materially weak culture of the Hispanic settlers. And just as there was no competition to their building practices, similarly in all other areas, the Americans triumphed. California was no exception to the general principle that economic and cultural dominance precedes military conquest. The fusion of advanced American and primitive Hispanic building traditions that began with the Monterey Style house is a powerful example of this rule. It represented a cultural accommodation in which ultimate Yankee supremacy was clearly prefigured. As one of the principal forces of cultural hegemony, architecture played a significant role in the larger struggle for control of California.

5. State Capitol Building, Benicia, 1852. Photograph by Chauncey A. Kirk.

IV

An Architectural Frontier

T he discovery of gold in the Sierra Nevada foothills in 1848, and the subsequent worldwide immigration that brought perhaps a hundred thousand people to California within two years, shattered any lingering hopes for an orderly transition from Mexican to American rule. For a brief time, however, the old provincial capital of Monterey, now the seat of the United States military government, continued its importance as the site for the convention called in the autumn of 1849 to draft a state constitution. The convention, with Thomas Oliver Larkin and Mariano Guadalupe Vallejo in prominent attendance, drafted a document in the established American constitutional tradition and proclaimed San Jose capital of what, within a year, became the thirty-first state to enter the Union. With this act of statehood, Monterey ceased to function importantly in the history of California.

The center of government, trade, and culture moved north and San Francisco began its nearly century-long dominance of the state's economic, intellectual, and artistic life. The city's supremacy derived from its strategic location at the entrance of the magnificent bay into which drain the river systems of the western slopes of the Sierra Nevada. The possession of that bay, rather than of the 160,000 square miles of what was considered at the time mostly wasteland, was the real reason for American annexation. Through the port commanding this bay passed most of the people and goods bound to and from California between 1849 and the arrival of the railroad twenty years later. In these formative American decades, California was thus a sea frontier, and its unprecedented international culture was a direct result of the heterogeneous immigration that reached San Francisco via the world's shipping lanes rather than the historic overland transit.

It is necessary to go back to the American colonial period to find a New World parallel to this overwhelmingly maritime immigration, as alien in character to the traditional American frontier as was the civilization it created to the stripped, survival frontier culture. The oceanic rather than continental nature of this immigration is graphically revealed in surviving daguerrotype views of San Francisco's waterfront in 1851, in which hundreds of ships lie at anchor, their masts forming a forest so dense as to obscure the view of the islands in the bay. The character of those who took passage in these vessels was described contemporaneously by Ralph Waldo Emerson as "an army of a hundred thousand picked volunteers, the ablest and keenest and boldest [from] New York, to Maine, to London . . . bringing tools, instruments, books, and framed houses."[1] The frequently applied phrase "California, the Great Exception" is particularly pertinent in explaining the twenty-year period commencing with the Gold Rush, when, as Emerson suggests, immigration was internationally selective. California was naturally one terminus of America's centuries-long westward movement; the exceptional element of this migration was the numerical acceleration and the qualitative selectivity of its earliest immigration as a result of world-wide reaction to the discovery of gold in the Sierra placers. Certain concurrent global conditions, such as the Irish Potato Famine, economic depression in France, the German Revolution of 1848, and the Taiping Rebellion in China, heightened this international response which, together with the restless adventuring spirit that accompanied America's expanding "Manifest Destiny," brought about what California historians call the Great Immigration.

This great, mid-century immigration was a brilliant exception to the historic pattern of westward expansion. Traditionally, American frontier culture has been an extension upon the last contiguous undeveloped area of the customs and ways of the most recent westward settlement. But California was an exception. The discovery of gold in 1848 suddenly opened up a frontier on the Pacific Ocean that, excepting Mormon country, was separated from the latest settlements west of the Missouri River by 1,500 miles of desert and wilderness. California was one of the first states that was not created out of the American agricultural frontier and that was without an established agrarian society directly behind it to shape the evolving culture. The lure of instant wealth and adventure, rather than an agrarian future, was the motivation for California's immigration in the 1850s and 1860s. In fact, California's present position as the nation's leading agricultural state was not achieved until the twentieth century. Economic problems, such as transportation, irrigation crop experimentation, and labor supply, had to be solved before the state's agricultural preeminence was assured.

There were other important aspects in which California's immigration differed markedly from traditional western settlement. Neither family-oriented nor community-directed, the immigration described by Emerson was exceptionally youthful, masculine, and single. In the decade of the 1850s, men outnumbered women five to one; the population was still seventy percent male in 1869 when the railway ended California's isolation as a sea frontier. Relatively unconcerned with a problematic future of settling homesteads, or raising crops and families, this was in fact California's first "now" generation: it sought in work instant achievement and in pleasure instant gratification. The general nature of the Great Immigration was summed up by the English traveler Frank Marryat in writing of San Francisco's population in 1853: "In no other community so limited could one find so many well-informed and clever men—men of all nations, who had added the advantages of travel to natural abilities and a liberal education."[2]

Although the Great Immigration was set in motion by events in 1848–1849, it was not limited to the period of the Gold Rush, but continued for two decades in a steady flow that deposited six hundred thousand people on a land that, prior to 1849, had a population of less than 15,000, excluding Indians. For architecture, the diversity and talent of this immigration was even more significant than its numbers. In 1850, twenty-five percent of California's population emigrated from outside the United States; by 1860, this minority had swelled to include forty percent of the state's inhabitants. With the completion of the Central Pacific Railroad nine years later, overseas immigration subsided and, particularly in the southern counties, its strikingly international character was diffused in subsequent overland migrations. Still, the average of foreign births to the total population for the entire last half of the nineteenth century was an impressive thirty percent. Architects in the Great Immigration followed closely this general pattern: one out of every three practicing in California in the 1850s and 1860s was foreign-born. These European-trained designers, half of whom were British, were instrumental in creating—in the two decades following the Gold Rush—a brilliant and innovative architecture unmatched on any previous American frontier.

The exceptional character of California's immigration in the 1850s and 1860s had a parallel in the state's economy, which was well grounded upon the wealth of placers and mines. The average annual production of gold in the 1850s is reckoned at 60 million dollars. In the following decade it fell roughly by half, but the discovery of the Comstock Lode in 1859 gave a silver supplement to the depleted California placers. While this "Big Bonanza" was mined in the territory of Nevada, the entire operation, from development capital to the supply of the miners, was a California project that put 400 million dollars into the pockets of San Francisco speculators and suppliers. This capital funded some of the most ambitious building schemes of the nineteenth century. With the lessening of gold production, many of the Argonnauts resumed traditional trades and professions, resulting in the development of industry and agriculture in the north and the revival of the cattle industry in the southern counties. California's historic shortage of manufactured goods—an economic disadvantage intensified by the Civil War and not really remedied until the completion of the transcontinental railroad in 1869—encouraged the growth of mills, factories, tanneries, shipyards, and even the manufacturing of munitions. The concentration of new industries in the San Francisco Bay region, because of population and port facilities, resulted in the rapid urbanization of that area which, in turn, promoted the cultural monopoly of northern California in the last half of the nineteenth century. But it was gold, and not the potential wealth of manufacturing and agriculture, that supplied the economic cornerstone of the state's first American generation. Gold created the wealth that built the instant metropolis of San Francisco, provided crucial fiscal support for the Union cause in the Civil War, and furnished the regional capital that constructed the Central Pacific Railroad and many allied industries. Sudden and vast mineral wealth also produced violence, inflation, instability, and reckless adventuring. These excesses in turn led to a search for order in all branches of life which, in terms of architecture, manifested itself in the great public buildings that housed the state's government, business, and religious worship.

The changeable quality of life in Gold Rush California is exemplified in the confusion that surrounded the location of the capital of the new state. Although the constitutional convention designated San Jose the seat of government, the legislature met there only for the 1850 and 1851 sessions. The choice of San Jose, located near the southern end of San Francisco Bay, pointed to the importance of both that body of water and the city, which in hardly a year was transformed from the straggling village of Yerba Buena into a metropolis excitedly known on four continents. The capitol building at San Jose continued the architectural compromise favored by New Englanders and their Hispanic allies in the decade prior to annexation: a two-story frame building with adobe walls, shingled roof, and balconied veranda. Dissatisfaction with this "unfinished box" led the restless legislators to transfer the state capital to the ambitiously conceived port "city" of Vallejo, some thirty miles northeast of San Francisco. This site proved even more

OLD FORMS ON A NEW LAND

desolate than San Jose. After only one week the government moved to Sacramento—just in time to be engulfed by the Great Flood of 1852. As Vallejo was still legally the capital of California, the lawmakers determined to meet there in January 1853. However, an uncomfortable month in the frame structure, whose only recorded distinction was the saloon and skittle alley in the basement (the "third house"), induced the legislators to proclaim nearby Benicia the "permanent" capital of California—and so it continued for two years. Laid out in 1847 by Larkin, General Vallejo, and Robert Semple on the north shore of Carquinez Straits with water access to San Francisco Bay, Benicia was a busy little town that contained the first United States Arsenal on the Pacific Coast and a recently constructed city hall noteworthy at the time for its dignity of design and practicality of plan (Plate 5). This structure, loaned to the legislature in 1853 and 1854, is historically misnomered the first California capitol.

The capitol at Benicia is the only survivor of the five buildings that served the peripatetic government between statehood in 1850 and the occupation of the present Sacramento edifice in 1869. It is shown in Plate 5 as restored to its original condition: a two-story brick structure with a sandstone foundation, recessed Doric colonnade, and pedimented gable. The architect is not known but he was, one presumes, familiar with the nearly identical St. James's Church in New York City, designed by Minard Lafever a generation earlier. Lafever, a self-taught architect with a reputation for common sense and practicality, had obvious appeal to those American architects of the Great Immigration who, by training and ability, more properly belonged to the ranks of carpenters. The particular book, *The Beauties of Modern Architecture* (1835), in which details (but not the elevation) from St. James's Church are published, was certainly prominent among the pattern books carried west by the forty-niners who, like builders everywhere in the United States in the nineteenth century, relied heavily upon manuals for instruction and inspiration. Indeed, the author of one of the most popular manuals, the New Englander Henry William Cleaveland, came to San Francisco in 1850 and for twenty years was a leader of the profession in California.

The capitol at Benicia, perhaps the earliest extant example of correct Greek Revival architecture in California, exerted a significant stylistic influence upon subsequent state, county, and municipal building. As an important expression on the farthest western frontier of the folk architecture of the eastern seaboard, it established that virtually all government buildings in the 1850s and 1860s in California would follow the nation in adhering to the Greek, as opposed to the

Roman, phase of that eighteenth-century European movement known as Classical Revival (neoclassicism), whose objective was a return to established principles based upon assumed laws of nature and reason. In America, Greek Revival represented the period of democracy between 1820 and 1860, and was particularly linked with the Greek struggle for independence from centuries of Turkish rule. Greek taste was especially prevalent in California mining towns, where the influence of San Francisco's major European-trained designers was negligible. As expected, old ways lingered longer outside the metropolis. The lag of approximately one generation that distinguished California culture generally from the eastern United States was very much evident in architecture outside San Francisco until at least the coming of the railroad. In their architectural colonialism, Californians were only following the national example, for the eastern practitioners whose work was so consistently imitated in the far west in the 1850s and 1860s were themselves following European trends—again with the same approximate time lag. Greek style in California was preeminently the work of the first generation of American designers. In their hands, it became a matter of decoration: a few simple elements taken from builders' manuals superimposed upon the traditional American wood-frame structure.

Despite the dignity and convenience of the Benicia capitol, the legislators were uneasy over the safety of public records housed in a building lacking fireproof vaults. When a suitable substitute was offered for legislative use in Sacramento, the capital was finally established in what then was the second city of California. The proffered structure, a square building with a full temple portico and domed lantern, burned in the summer of 1854 and was replaced early in the following year by a new one that served the state until 1869, when the present capitol was finally completed. Although stylistically the building that functioned as the fifth statehouse continued the entrenched Greek tradition, the strong affinity with the austere established United States models was replaced by an Old World sumptuousness. For the architect was David Farquharson, a highly trained Scot who arrived in San Francisco in 1850. As was earlier noted, foreign-born Californians consisted of thirty percent of the state's non-Indian population during the second half of the nineteenth century. That same ratio prevailed among the professional designers of international origins, half of whom were British. Chief among the latter were Farquharson and William Patton, a forty-niner who was trained in the London office of Sir Gilbert Scott, one of the foremost practitioners in England at mid century.

OLD FORMS ON A NEW LAND

6. Hibernia Society and Bank Building, San Francisco, 1857. Peter Portois, architect. *Architectural Record,* XX (1906), p. 22. Destroyed. Courtesy of the Bancroft Library.

Farquharson and Patton, together with their continental colleagues, the German Victor Hoffman and the Belgian Peter Portois, designed many of the celebrated and lost landmarks of old San Francisco, including Wright's Bank (1854), Globe Hotel (1857), Temple Emanu-El (1865–1866), Bank of California (1866–1867), and Starr King Chapel (1864), the last named for the Unitarian minister whose oratory is credited as crucial in holding California to the Union cause in the Civil War.[3] In a historical sense, the most significant of the European Gold Rush architects was Peter Portois. If he can be believed, Portois designed, in 1851, the first work in the United States by a graduate of France's famed Ecole des Beaux-Arts.[4] Portois' earliest San Francisco commissions are unrecorded; their nature can be inferred, however, by reference to his seminal design for the Hibernia Society and Bank Building (Plate 6), a remarkable forerunner of that academic classicism traditionally held to owe its American beginnings to northeastern examples dating twenty or more years later.

Nothing remains of this pioneer architecture (Plates 6 and 7) that, in the opinion of Henry Adams, gave San Francisco "more style than any town in the east."[5] The buildings are known only through a handful of photographs, as their architects are known only from brief obituaries. The native-born critic, Bruce Porter, whose boyhood was passed in the shadow of what in his maturity he described as the "really notable buildings [that] were erected in San Francisco . . . between 1850 and 1870," was one of the first to speculate upon their origins.[6] Because he could find no contemporary models in America comparable to them—their architects' names, birthplaces, and sources of professional training then largely unknown—Porter was forced to conclude that the buildings were commissioned in London and Paris, the European capitals in which he received his own artistic training. Agnes Foster Buchanan, agreeing with Porter's estimate of the "intelligence and taste" of San Francisco's European-born designers and of the "grace and power" of their work, more accurately sought its source in the Great Immigration:[7]

They were . . . the first business buildings erected in the United States which were both exotic and interesting—buildings which were the product of an alien tradition, yet which retained under American surroundings a certain propriety and a positive charm.

In their solidity and monumentality, these architectural manifestations of California's first great international immigration represented the third stage in the

7. Montgomery Block, San Francisco, 1853. Gordon P. Cummings, architect. G. R. Gardon, *San Francisco Album* (San Francisco, 1856), p. 15. Destroyed. Courtesy of the Bancroft Library.

development of San Francisco. They supplanted, within a few years, the canvas and prefabricated buildings of the Gold Rush, and the austere one or two-story brick structures in the Greek style which represented the first response to the devastating fires that swept the city in the early 1850s. Usually four stories in height, massively constructed in stone and beautifully sculptured, the great business blocks and hotels that rose almost miraculously amid the haste, confusion, and gaudy magnificence of San Francisco's first American generation were in a style generally characterized as Mannerist. But in the context of mid-nineteenth century California, this Old World nomenclature is perhaps best rendered as Victorian Italianate. As used in San Francisco by the European-trained architects, the style was largely decorative: an effect of richness, movement, and depth achieved through the imposition of surface ornament upon an ordered and formal structure. Although rooted strongly in European tradition, these vanished buildings were sufficiently separated from their sources to assume the sudden, changing, and extravagant character of San Francisco's gold and silver decades. This was an exuberant time with an exuberant architecture wonderfully representative of the Great Immigration that created, on a rich and isolated frontier, one of the most extraordinary and neglected chapters in America's cultural history.

Building in the decades between the Gold Rush and the completion of the transcontinental railroad in 1869 reflected the talented, transitory, youthful, and masculine quality of the Great Immigration. During these twenty years, the state's immigrant population had an average ratio of six men to one woman. The important building projects of these decades—hotels, government buildings, banks, and office blocks—generally conformed to the masculine and adventuring nature of California in its early period of statehood. However, the existence of important church architecture among the public buildings in this restless era of gold and silver dominance attests to the strong character of the pioneering clergy. Foremost among them were Starr King, for whose San Francisco congregation William Patton designed a Gothic fantasy, and William Kip, the New York-born and Yale-educated churchman who arrived in 1854 to become the first Episcopal bishop of California. With the entire state his diocese, Kip's influence upon California church architecture extended beyond the great metropolis to the mining towns and the developing agricultural communities. For those rural areas, Bishop Kip encouraged the building of simple board and batten churches in the Gothic Revival style that owed their design to models that Richard Upjohn published in a pattern book prepared expressly for small mission churches.

St. James's in Sonora (Plate 8), the second of the extant churches constructed in the Sierra foothills under Kip's episcopate, is an outstanding example of how eastern building forms followed America's westward migration. For not only is every element in St. James's design contained in *Upjohn's Rural Architecture* (1852), but its board and batten construction conforms to the northeastern wood tradition that proved adaptable to frontier conditions from the old Northwest all the way to California. Board and batten construction had appeared in California prior to annexation, but was not commonly employed until after the Gold Rush. Among the most interesting early examples of this method of construction were the rows of pre-fabricated cottages, complete with picket fences, that were shipped around Cape Horn from Boston, erected in San Francisco's Happy Valley in 1850, and described by Bishop Kip as "neat and pretty cottages."[8] Board and batten construction was deemed appropriate by American gothicists for church designs because of the visual sense of height conveyed by the fluctuant and vertical thrust of the material, especially in relation to the requisite octagonal or square tower. This type of construction was inevitably the building material for St. James's, the "little red church," constructed in Sonora in 1859 in response to a petition to the bishop from the community's leading citizens.

The church, whose site was the abandoned workings of one of the richest yielding pocket mines in California, was erected under the supervision of the Reverend John Gassman, a native of Norway reputed to have been skilled in the building trades. The salient features are revealed in Plate 8: board and batten construction, pitched shingle roof, lateral tower, plain lancet windows, and decorative buttresses. The only incongruous element is the pair of hoods over the doors; they were not a part of the original design but were added after a fire in 1868. The church walls still bear the deep red stain prescribed by Upjohn. The design, both simple and churchly, met the frontier criterion of utility. It had been pragmatically tested prior to publication and proved as suitable on the West Coast as it had been in the rural parishes of northwestern New York.

Surviving churches built in the Upjohn vernacular range along the California coast from the spectacularly sited Presbyterian Church (1867) in Mendocino to the thrice-moved St. Mark's (1875) in Santa Barbara. Utilizing the design of buildings erected in the Northeast, these churches are modest reflections of the Gothic Revival, which like the earlier Greek Revival, was carried to California by pioneer patrons and builders who superimposed a few decorative forms upon traditional North American woodframe construction. The style's hallmark, clearly evident in

8. St. James's Episcopal Church, Sonora, 1859. Photograph by Chauncey A. Kirk.

St. James's Sonora, was the pointed arch. The battlement was another of the medieval motifs used in a purely decorative sense; a representative example still surmounts the bell tower of the Mariposa County Courthouse (1854). In this latter building, elements of both Greek and Gothic revivals are combined in an architectural accommodation not uncommon to California in the decade following annexation. The pioneer builders also followed the eastern practice of limiting medieval tracery to gingerbread cutouts—known as verge boards—applied to the vertical triangular ends of steep gables. It was from the widespread application of verge boards that the style acquired the popular designation of "Carpenters' Gothic." Two survivors of this vernacular are the prefabricated cottages shipped from Boston in 1849 and reassembled just outside the pueblo of Sonoma for General Mariano Vallejo and in Benicia for John Frisbie.

When Gothic-style houses were actually designed in California, as in the case of the extant Moss Cottage in Oakland in 1864 by the New York-born architect, Stephen H. Williams, they generally followed the model developed by Alexander Jackson Davis and popularized by the landscape architect Andrew Jackson Downing in his many publications. The latter's pattern books, particularly *The Architecture of Country Houses* (1850), were available in San Francisco bookstores after 1852. Reviewed in the *Alta California* early in the following year, this manual was especially recommended to the San Francisco building profession for the ease with which Davis's designs could be executed in redwood. With the discovery and logging of the vast redwood groves in Mendocino, Humboldt, and Del Norte counties, this native material quickly replaced costlier imports, such as iron and cut stone from China and prefabricated structures from Massachusetts, England, and Australia.

The unquestioned acceptance of eastern building forms and prevailing modes by native Californians and native Americans alike extended equally to the Chinese immigrant. This is forcefully seen in the conversion of a Gothic Revival board-and-batten church in Sacramento into a "Chinese Chapel" in the early years after annexation.[9] Complete with barge-board lace work, lancet windows, and a belfry bristling with crockets, the original Christian church, assembled about 1850, was adapted to Buddhist worship without architectural modification. Such outward adaptation—in this case consisting only in the removal of the cross and the addition of a scroll in native characters—was typical of the utilization of almost every nineteenth century building by the Chinese minority and reflected the basic conditions of their life in California: impermanent, isolated, and devoid of political or even civic participation.

By the time of the conversion of the Gothic church in Sacramento to Buddhist services, the Chinese accounted for one out of every ten Californians. Agitation against their numbers, contemporaneously called the "Celestial invasion," had widened into racial conflict. This animosity was in direct contrast to the early contacts in which the Chinese were welcomed as much-needed laborers in agriculture, fishing, laundries, and restaurants, and as household servants. But the financial panic of 1854, together with the depletion of the gold placers, sent miners by the thousands to San Francisco and Sacramento in search of work and the generous receiving mood toward the Chinese was sharply altered. Competition among the work force was especially severe in the building trades, in which the Chinese were now active as carpenters, cabinetmakers, carvers, brick makers, and laborers. The presence of so many Chinese laborers in this area accounted for some of the worst racial incidents in California's first quarter-century of statehood.

Despite employment of Chinese in the construction trades, they rarely influenced the design or outward appearance of buildings erected for, or adapted to, their own usage. Their tendency to accept Western building standards was early and frequently observed. Commenting on the absence of any "quaint" Chinese architecture in San Francisco, a visitor in 1875 noted that the building, which housed the most important "Joss chamber" of the city's fifteen places of Buddhist and Taoist worhsip, was thus identifiable only by "a little display of tinsel on the balcony" and a pair of "artificially animated" dragons flanking the door frame.[10] A study of photographs indicates that San Francisco's famed old Chinatown (the present one is entirely the result of rebuilding after 1906) was distinguishable from the surrounding commercial districts only by the relatively rare use of ornamental balconies, decorated poles, hanging lanterns of paper or bronze, signs, and porcelain dragons.

Far from the metropolis, however, in the mining towns, fishing villages, and railroad encampments, there were exceptions to the architectural accommodationusually practiced by the first generations of Orientals in California. These exceptions occurred in the construction by the Chinese of their Joss houses. The term Joss house (pidgin English from Portuguese *deus*) was used in reference to the temple or shrine that was generally a part of every Chinese settlement. In the construction of these places of worship in the mining and rural areas, the Chinese often made a deliberate effort to effect in the design of the building an

9. Chinese Joss House, Weaverville, 1852–1853; reconstructed 1869–1895.
Courtesy of the Bancroft Library.

outward expression of its purpose and antecedents. Among the few extant Joss houses are the temple in Oroville dating from 1863 and the reconstruction, from a decade later, in Weaverville of the shrine Won Lim Miao—the Temple of the Forest and Clouds (Plate 9). The latter structure, preserved as a State Historical Monument, was originally built in 1852–1853 when Weaverville had an Oriental population of perhaps 2500 and Chinatown occupied two blocks on both sides of the main street of what is probably the best preserved of California's old mining towns. Still maintained as a place of worship, Won Lim Miao was constructed of the local material: wood rather than stone. Its furnishings were salvaged from periodic fires and consist largely of the original carvings, panels, gongs, lanterns, and banners shipped from China to San Francisco in 1854 and transported by steamer up the Sacramento River to Colusa, and from there by mule to Weaverville.

The state Capitol in Sacramento (Plate 10), the last great building project undertaken in the period between the Gold Rush and the arrival of the railroad, can serve as a representation of the backgrounds, training, and regional relationships which determined the American phase of the international architecture that distinguished northern California in the fifties and sixties. The original design—that which was judged best in the competition of 1860—was the work of Miner Butler, who arrived in San Francisco from his native Georgia in 1849. Although Butler was awarded the prize, the corresponding post of Superintendent of Construction was given to another forty-niner, Reuben Clark, who is thought to have considerably altered the original design.

Clark began his professional life as a carpenter on the Maine statehouse (1829–1832), the last of Charles Bulfinch's great public commissions and one that established the format for almost all subsequent state capitol construction: hemispherical dome and columnar frontispiece, and, whenever possible, the use of granite as the building material. Upon Clark's death in 1866, the work was taken over by Gordon Cummings, whose Montgomery Block (Plate 7) is generally held to have been the most splendid and important building in California prior to the completion of the Capitol. Cummings, a New Yorker, is said to have been trained in England; certainly he was one of the most experienced architects in the Gold Rush. When the Capitol was officially occupied in 1869, Cummings was succeeded by the state architect Albert Bennett, under whose supervision the building was completed five years later at a cost of more than one and one-half million dollars.

10. State Capitol, Sacramento, 1860–1874. Photograph by Chauncey A. Kirk.

The Capitol represents a fusion of several of the major architectural elements colonized in California as a result of the Great Immigration: the American Classical Revival and the mid-nineteenth century European amalgam of Mannerism and Baroque generally known in the vagaries of architectural nomenclature as Italianate. Historically, the California Capitol is important as the furthest western example of a national architecture formulated by Bulfinch over a period of forty years and carried south and west by Yankee builders. Reuben Clark was an outstanding participator in this process of architectural nationalization, for, excepting the area of the Middle West, he was involved in statehouse construction in every major section of the United States. He was, moreover, unusual in his devotion to the professional standards of his time, bringing to the task of completing the Sacramento Capitol great singleness of purpose. As a result of laboring day and night on the working drawings, worrying endlessly over delays in the shipment and quality of materials, and disheartened by continual and often petty legislative criticism, his sanity gave out and he died in 1866 in the state asylum. Although Clark's work has been substantially modified over the last century, the Capitol remains essentially what the New England designer had intended: an architectural statement of California's adherence to the Union cause in a period of divided loyalties and deep uncertainties.

The creation of a transcontinental railroad line was an important national goal. Its completion in 1869 ended California's geographic isolation. Heretofore, California had been a sea frontier whose contacts were not with the traditional American West but the world's principal cities: Vera Cruz, Lima, Valparaiso, Honolulu, Sitka, and Boston in the Spanish-Mexican period and Boston, New York, London, Paris, Hamburg, Sydney, and Hong Kong in the initial American decades. Upon this oceanic frontier, a half-dozen cultures contested for supremacy. Their impact upon building was an international architecture that, although as yet little studied, introduced academic classicism into America at least a generation before its appearance on the East Coast. The basis for California's extraordinary architectural significance in the period before the coming of the railroad was mineral wealth and a numerically large and racially diverse immigration. With the material means to encourage the arts and the cosmopolitan talents to create it, California building in the first twenty years of statehood was much more than a regional expression of northeastern stylistic revivals. It was the most brilliant architecture raised upon any American frontier.

11. Italianate Row Houses, San Francisco, ca. 1878. Photograph by Greg Alcorn.

V

In The Mainstream

The completion of the transcontinental railroad did not produce the instant prosperity and progress promised by its builders. Instead, the merging of the state's economy with that of the nation coincided with declines both in gold production and immigration, and the regional backlash of the Panic of 1873. Prosperity was further hindered by such longer term deterrents as recurring drought, lack of coal resources, high tariffs, and the opening of new frontiers for capital exploitation in the Klondike and Alaska. Yet California's agricultural supremacy was predestined. Even before the railway, the state was well on the way to achieving its boast as "the granary of the world." The penetration of the railroad into the Central Valley and the southern counties, together with the development of irrigation and crops, resulted in the world's most profitable farming operations. The land and the climate, a diversified immigration, and the development of mechanized agriculture worked together to produce an agrarian system that steadily advanced through the central and southern portions of the state. Thus, regional factors and national technology—such as the invention of the refrigerator car—played complementary roles in the transition from gold to agriculture as the state's principal economic asset.

Although the southern portion of California did not gain economic dominance until the middle of the next century, many of the contributing factors—health and land boom, citrus and petroleum industry—had their early growth with the coming of the railroad. The Southern Pacific (a development of the railroad that formed the western link with the transcontinental system) reached Los Angeles in 1876, precipitating a Health Rush that resulted in the first major hotel construction in southern California. A decade later, the Santa Fe broke the Southern

Pacific's monopoly and began a propaganda and rate war with its rival that brought a one-way ticket from Kansas City to Los Angeles to a low of one dollar. The subsequent land boom led to the creation of some sixty new town sites and the sale of more than thirty-five million dollars worth of Los Angeles real estate.

An important element in the land boom was the enormous interest and activity in a renewed and improved citrus fruit culture. Prior to 1870, a citrus grove was a rarity; within a decade and a half there were more than 2 million bearing trees with an annual production of 2,250 carloads of oranges. The modern citrus fruit industry resulted in the establishment in California of a new kind of cooperative town development that transformed both the economy and social life of the Los Angeles area. Examples of the carefully organized villages of the mid-seventies, with their strong urban and Yankee character, were Pomona, Pasadena, and Riverside. It was at the latter town that modern irrigation and the seedless navel orange were introduced into southern California.

Along with the growth of a thriving citrus culture came exploitation of the state's oil resources. At the height of the land boom, petroleum production was 700,000 barrels annually; by the end of the century, this had been increased to 4 million. The Oil Rush of the nineties was conducted with many of the devices which proved so successful in the land boom, which, if not distinguished by an overabundance of veracity, proved extremely effective in opening up new fields in road paving, locomotive fuel, lighting, and heating.

When the land boom collapsed in 1889, a few of the new towns were left without a single inhabitant. Despite an immediate depression in building and a temporary deflation in Los Angeles County real estate, this period was responsible for revolutionary changes in every section of southern California. The land boom marked the near extinction of the rancho and the increased submergence of Spanish-Mexican culture by an avalanche of Anglo-Saxon immigration. The old dependence upon cattle raising was replaced by the rapidly expanding citrus fruit and petroleum industries, the development of the building trades, and the growth of resort and health communities.

Like the earlier generation of Gold Rush builders, the American architects who came west after 1869 in pursuit of careers, health, and sunshine brought with them a high average of talent, training, and experience. Again as in the fifties and sixties, most were from the northeastern United States. The most prominent of these at the time of immigration was A. Page Brown, who graduated from Cornell University and served an apprenticeship with the leading New York firm of

McKim, Mead and White. Among those Brown encouraged to join him in setting up his San Francisco office in 1889 were the New York born Albert Schweinfurt, one of four architect-sons of a German woodworker, and Willis Polk, master rebuilder of San Francisco after the fire of 1906 and one of the most influential architects to practice in California in the first two decades of the twentieth century. In 1887 the New Englander, John Galen Howard, immigrated to California, bringing with him an unrivaled professional education at Massachusetts Institute of Technology and the Ecole des Beaux-Arts, and experience as a draftsman for Henry Hobson Richardson. Whatever his original intentions, Howard stayed only a year in the West, where he was among the first to recognize, in the ruins of the Franciscan missions, the potential source for a native regional revival. After returning to New York to work with the premier American firm of McKim, Mead and White, Howard came back to California in 1901 to supervise the implementation of the Hearst Plan for the University of California and to head that institution's newly created department of architecture.

The health and land rushes of the seventies and eighties resulted in the first important colonization of architects in southern California. Among the earliest of these were the New Yorkers Sumner P. Hunt, a leading exponent of Mediterranean architecture on the West Coast; J. A. Walls, later a partner in the pioneer Los Angeles firm of Keysor and Morgan, who arrived in 1888 after three years in Richardson's Boston office; and Frederick L. Roehrig, Cornell graduate and designer of the surviving Green Hotel Annex (1898). From the Middle West came Arthur B. Benton, whose Mission Inn in Riverside (begun 1902), is a masterpiece of its style, and Myron Hunt and Elmer Grey, partners in a distinguished Los Angeles office but long and influential residents of Pasadena.

Although far fewer foreign-born and trained architects took part in the southern California health and real estate booms than had participated in the Gold Rush, their numbers included such important designers as the Englishmen William Weeks, president of the southern California chapter of the American Institute of Architects, and Ernest Coxhead, Silver Medalist of the Royal Institute of British Architects, whose significant California career began in Los Angeles in 1886. From Canada came James Reid, a student of McGill University and the Beaux-Arts, and architect of the famous Hotel del Coronado (1886–1888). The Norwegian Joachim Mathisen, trained as a civil engineer in Germany, was one of A. Page Brown's numerous proteges and an influential figure in the development of the Mission Revival.

The second great immigration of architects reflected the fundamental new fact of California life: the railroad. Just as rail linkage between east and west brought the state's economy into the national mainstream, so architecture increasingly represented American taste. Such foreign influences as were felt in California came generally, as they did to the nation at large, from the East Coast. The immediate result was a cycle of revivals which temporarily reduced the state to a provincial mirror for every capricious national style change. By the end of the century, however, the railroad had brought to California a half dozen of its most distinguished designers. Among these were several who were to create an architecture that, no matter how tentative, represented for the first time an appreciation of the land and its history.

This crucial phase in the development of California architecture began in 1888 with the arrival of Bernard Maybeck in San Francisco and ended five years later with the immigration of Charles and Henry Greene and Irving Gill to southern California for health reasons. Maybeck was trained in his youth as a craftsman, graduated from the Paris Beaux-Arts, and worked in the New York office of Carrère and Hastings. He was the first of only two Californians to receive the Gold Medal of the American Institute of Architects. The Greene brothers came from a distinguished New England family, studied at Massachusetts Institute of Technology, and apprenticed in several prestigious Boston offices. Gill, a New Yorker like Maybeck, was apprenticed to the Chicago architect, Louis Sullivan. These men were the inheritors of the great pioneer architects of the 1850s and 1860s. Their average age was twenty-five; their training was exceptional even by European standards; and their experience in leading eastern offices reflected the major orientation of American economic and cultural life after the Civil War. In our times the work of these men has become legendary.

In the period of the California building boom of the 1880s, the practice of architecture was well into its second generation and a strong northern leadership in the field had been established. San Francisco architects, of whom there were more than seventy-five registered, dominated the western profession. In 1880, they began publication of their own journal, *California Architect and Building News,* which for twenty years not only reported regional information but also transmitted pictorially the latest eastern styles. At the same time, the San Francisco chapter of the American Institute of Architects initiated classes in freehand drawing, "practical architecture," modeling, and mathematics. The method of instruction was based upon that of the Beaux-Arts as learned by the youthful California

         OLD FORMS ON A NEW LAND

immigrants who had trained with Richardson and Charles Follen McKim. These classes merged in 1893 with the San Francisco Art Institute, then quartered in the Mark Hopkins Mansion on Nob Hill and, after 1895, were distinguished by the presence of Bernard Maybeck. At about the same time, Maybeck began teaching a drawing class at the University of California; he also offered private instruction in architecture in his Berkeley house to a number of young Californians, such as Arthur Brown, Jr., and Julia Morgan, both of whom completed their training in Paris and returned to the Bay Area to long and distinguished practices in the following century.

Despite the increasing influence of regional professional schools and local Beaux-Arts societies, the most important phase in the education of the young American architect continued to be the apprenticeship. In California in the late nineteenth century, apprenticeships were served almost entirely in San Francisco offices, especially those of the pioneer European-trained architects David Farquharson and William Mooser. Farquharson's students included John J. Clark and Clinton Day, who eventually became partners, and the native-born Edward Swain, who left his master in 1877 to begin a practice that led to a partnership with A. Page Brown and, after the latter's early death in 1895, the assumption of what was then the most progressive office on the West Coast. The most important of Mooser's apprentices was Albert Pissis. He was brought to California from Mexico at the age of six, studied at the Beaux-Arts, and pursued a brilliant San Francisco practice in the nineties. Among other native Californians exposed to this growing body of professional schools and practitioners were Walter Bliss and William Faville, who completed their architectural educations at MIT and served apprenticeships with McKim, Mead and White before returning to San Francisco in 1898 to form a partnership that resulted in some of the finest West Coast examples of American Renaissance architecture.

Through boom and bust, redwood continued as California's principal building material. Although historian Hubert Howe Bancroft's assertion that there was not a single residence of brick or stone in San Francisco in the late 1880s is an obvious exaggeration, nine-tenths of the structures of that city were frame—a higher percentage than in any other American metropolis. The eminently appropriate quality of wood construction in a land whose chief natural phenomenon other than sunshine is the earthquake has never been a major consideration in its almost universal use in California domestic building. Wood was used not out of fear but because it was relatively cheap, readily available, perfectly suited the temperate climate, and for centuries had been the primary North American building material.

The wooden row houses illustrated in Plate 11 are representative examples of the state's immediate post-railroad architecture. Dating from the late 1870s, these San Francisco dwellings exemplify the regional variation of the eastern brownstone. The significant differences are wood construction and the great prominence given to the bay window. The wood, of course, was redwood; construction was the Chicago or Balloon frame system that revolutionized the California housing industry after the Civil War. The Chicago or Balloon frame method radically departed from traditional construction by substituting for heavy timbers, which were held together by painstakingly cut tenon and mortise, a light skeleton of two-by-four-inch studs upon which clapboards were simply nailed. This method, so named because its apparent fragility suggested the structure would blow away with the wind, was the most important American contribution to building technology in the first half of the nineteenth century. It was dependent upon standardized sawn lumber and machine-made nails, both of which were in common supply on the West Coast by 1869. Balloon frame construction was enthusiastically accepted in California by reason of the temperate climate, a chronic housing shortage, and a building profession new enough to be open to innovative, and especially cost-cutting, ideas.

The importance given the bay window was one of several significant design changes in the western domestication of the eastern brownstone. Upon this feature, the state's first vernacular architecture was fearlessly grounded. Almost every California house built in the last quarter of the nineteenth century was distinguished by at least one such window. This was particularly so in San Francisco, where bay-windowed row houses constitute that city's most treasured Victorian heritage. But their kind was not limited to urban situations. Thousands of dwellings such as those shown in Plate 11 were constructed between the late sixties and early eighties in rural towns and in the countryside as well as the Bay Area metropolis. Usually two-storied but often only one, they stretched in urban rows, stood in romantic solitude in surburban parks, or were planted in vertical isolation on remote ranches.

Ultimately derived from the farmhouses of the Italian countryside, this dignified and even severe style is known as Italianate. It reached California by the traditional nineteenth-century route: first, by evolutionary development in early Victorian England, then through introduction by means of pattern books in the eastern United States in the 1840s, and finally, after the usual two-generation time lag, with the westward journey in the memory of immigrant-architects. The outstanding characteristics of the style as it evolved into a California row vernacular are evident in Plate 11: verticality enhanced by a richly bracketed parapet (hiding the traditional gable roof), a heavily articulated entrance porch surmounted by a single window and a "squeezed" pediment, and tiers of slanted bay windows with flanking colonettes.

In addition to wood construction and expanded bay windows, the Italianate style underwent one other significant transformation in the course of its western evolution. The somber colors of the eastern brownstones gave way first to white, beige, or gray and then, in time, to "mustard yellow," "Indian red," and "verdant green." Thus, excepting for the present-day eccentricity of picking out architectural details in contrasting colors, the California "Victorians" early qualified for their contemporary reputation as "Painted Ladies."

The creation of an urban vernacular in the last quarter of the nineteenth century was effected only through mass technology and financing. The imported Balloon frame method provided the ultimate in simplified construction; the power-driven saws and lathes of the regional mill works supplied standardized doors and windows and frames as well as the entablatures, scrolls, and panels which were the distinguishing features of the California Victorians. Such structural economies were matched by a basic uniformity in plan and facade that remained constant despite the superficial stylistic evolution from Italianate to Queen Anne-Eastlake. The same necessary conditions pertained in financing. Local real estate associations and builders' alliances constructed thousands of houses similar to those in Plate 11 by means of craft specialization and large-scale financing. The typical San Francisco row house could be purchased for about two thousand dollars; in Los Angeles, the model sold for half that amount. Cottages financed and constructed under similar circumstances cost between five hundred and one thousand dollars. Such mass methods of construction and financing provided not only inexpensive but also efficiently planned, well lighted, and comfortable housing for a large segment of the population traditionally ignored by the architectural profession.

The picturesque, but somewhat austere, Italianate proved inadequate to the stylistic demands of a frontier society entering upon its final and most exuberant phase. Surprising though it seems today, one hundred years ago the Italianate was attacked in the regional press as "insultingly plain"—a defect that California architects remedied by an enthusiastic espousal of the latest imported styles:

Queen Anne and Eastlake. The former, based upon the imaginative eclecticism of Richard Norman Shaw and derived loosely from Elizabethan, Dutch, and William and Mary elements, was characterized by changing surfaces of brick, shingle, and tile, with elaborate chimneys and gabled roofs. Eastlake, an architectural adaptation of the sawed and incised furniture designs of Sir Charles Eastlake, was, like the misnamed Queen Anne, introduced to America at the Philadelphia Centennial Exposition of 1876. As used in the irreverent hands of California's late Victorians, however, these imported components were simply, and haphazardly, tacked onto the facade of the traditional timbered house with its ubiquitous bay window.

To appreciate fully the errant playfulness with which regional architects used the latest English styles as well as other contemporary ones, such as the French Second Empire, today one must travel to Eureka, the late nineteenth-century capital of the redwood logging industry, located in the extreme northern part of the state. Here, the captain of that industry, William Carson, built what is properly regarded as one of the finest Victorian residences in America (Plate 12). The Carson House was constructed in 1884–1885 and, after sheltering three generations of Carsons, is now lovingly preserved as a private club. It was somewhat altered after the builder's death in 1912, when his daughter-in-law removed most of the decorative iron work, roof finials, and other exterior elements as well as chandeliers and furniture. Essentially, however, the house stands as its builder intended, an awesome monument to a pioneering society whose self-confidence is demonstrated in a structure of great architectural daring.

Samuel and Joseph Cather Newsom, the designers of the Carson House, were characteristic exceptions to the professional traditions which created California's first American half-century of building. As children of a nurseryman with uncertain connections in the building trades, the Newsoms were brought to San Francisco from Canada in 1861. Their training was undoubtedly at the hands of two elder brothers, who, in the informality of a frontier society, called themselves "Architects and Superintendents of Building." But whatever Samuel and Joseph Cather Newsom lacked in eastern training and Beaux-Arts assumptions, their education was sufficient to their Ruskinian sense of architecture as ornament. The brothers enunciated their theory of design in one of many self-advertisements: "the degree of ornamentation will be governed, more or less, by the size of the builder's purse."[1] The Carson House truly fulfilled this dictum. It demonstrated better than

12. Carson House, Eureka, 1884–85. Samuel and Joseph Newsom, architects. Photograph by Greg Alcorn.

any other of the Newsoms's numerous and exotic creations how instinctive was their skill in translating pattern-book borrowing into magnificent reality.

Some critics, raised in the stern school of functionalism, have decried the Carson House as a monument to the Victorians's sham substantiality and artistic confusion. Increasingly, however, a generation of nostalgists have found in its spacious rooms, hidden nooks, and sunny hallways, an alternative to the unimaginative, cramped, and bleak dimensions of so much of contemporary housing. Similarly, Californians living in times of diminishing expectations see the house as an embodiment of plans, hopes, and promises as grand as the redwoods from which its timbers were taken. Extravagant the Carson House certainly is, but also reassuringly solid and comfortable and comforting.

At the same time the Newsoms were demonstrating in California the seemingly limitless possibilities of what they construed to be Queen Anne, a group of eastern architects were introducing a sophisticated Boston and New York clientele to what subsequently has been labeled the Shingle Style. This style developed out of a renewed interest in colonial building resulting from the Philadelphia Centennial Exposition of 1876. It was expected that the hundredth anniversary of the Declaration of Independence would turn Americans in search of roots back to their colonial past; what was not anticipated was their discovery of an architectural ideal not in the trim, almost formal eighteenth-century models but in the much earlier, weathered, roughly shingled houses which were then still commonly seen in remote New England villages. The exact circumstances by which such architectural innovators as H. H. Richardson and Stanford White discovered these seventeenth-century prototypes are not known. Beginning in the late 1870s, however, there was a revival of early American building forms distinguished principally by low, box-like forms, exterior walls of unpainted shingles, and small, many-paned windows. To these authentic elements were appended verandas, conical or hexagonal towers, and occasionally, Queen Anne flourishes in the form of a Palladian window, cartouche of plaster, and Jacobean chimney. The style, which derived ultimately from the folk architecture of that part of southeastern England that supplied the first great Puritan immigrations, was easily assimilated into California's now dominant wood building tradition.

The complex eastern shingle house brought to San Francisco by A. Page Brown and Willis Polk underwent a rapid transformation into what has now become know as the Bay Area Tradition. The forces that shaped this transmutation were history, climate, clientele, and the versatility with which the style was adapted to regional building needs. The first redwood shingles used in California construction seem to have been cut north of San Francisco Bay in 1833; a few years later the shingle roof had become a hallmark of the Monterey Style house; by 1850 almost every structure in the mining communities embodied the use of shingles in some phase of construction. But California's historic shingled structures, uniformly simple and small in scale, represented a tradition generally at variance with the rambling eastern "cottages" so rich in turrets and towers, segmental bays, and elaborate dormers. Their vast, embracing porches, designed for Atlantic seaboard summer communities, were inappropriate to the Bay Area climate and its decidedly urban style of life. Because the regional style builders were professors, lawyers, and musicians instead of bankers, stockbrokers, and sportsmen, with affiliations characterized by the Sierra Club rather than the Tuxedo Club, the Bay Area Tradition was one of greatly reduced scale and with a tendency toward what its early apologist, Charles Keeler, called "The Simple Home."

The exceptional versatility with which Californians extended the Shingle Style to multiple building requirements was another significant element in the creation of the Bay Area Tradition. On the East Coast the style was limited largely to domestic construction; in California it was employed with astonishing variety as to range and form. John Galen Howard adapted it to university complexes such as the School of Architecture at Berkeley; Bernard Maybeck designed great shingled edifices to house schools, clubs, and even a gymnasium. Finally, it was early adapted to ecclesiastical purposes and the first results, such as A. C. Schweinfurt's Unitarian Church in Berkeley (1898), and the dozen surviving religious edifices of Coxhead, comprise the most original regional development of the Shingle Style.

Ernest Coxhead, son of an English schoolmaster, was trained in the Royal Academy of Fine Arts and the Royal Institute of British Architects before immigrating to Los Angeles in 1886. His knowledge of English ecclesiastical architecture, as well as his debt to the eastern Shingle Style, are evident in the southern California churches he designed for the Episcopal Diocese between 1887 and 1889, four of which survive in varying states of alteration. But it was not until Coxhead moved his office to San Francisco in 1890 and became identified with the group gathered around A. Page Brown that his personal style became dramatically evident. This phase is particularly pronounced in St. Peter's Episcopal Church, Red Bluff (Plate 13), consecrated in 1892.

A comparison of this building with St. James's Episcopal Church (Plate 8)

13. St. Peter's Episcopal Church, Red Bluff, 1892. Ernest Coxhead, architect. Courtesy of the Tehama County Library.

demonstrates both the pervasiveness of wood construction in California ecclesiastical architecture throughout the entire last half of the nineteenth century as well as the great advance in design sophistication resulting in part from current English influences such as the Arts and Crafts Movement. The romantic intensity conveyed in the use of materials and details in St. Peter's gives what one critic has called a "taut abstractness" to the essentially simple design—the most striking feature of which is the "witch hat" tower Coxhead employed concurrently in St. John's Episcopal Church in Monterey.[2] Another significant design element is the tiny but exquisite star window wonderously set against rough cut shingles on each side of the porch. This is both an indication of Coxhead's celebrated wit and a signal of the new nativist movement, the Mission Revival, only recently promoted from the office of A. Page Brown with the California Building for the World's Columbian Exposition at Chicago.

Like most of the Victorian styles domesticated in California in the last half of the nineteenth century, the Shingle reached its apogee in the San Francisco Bay Area, where, indeed, it continues to be favored as the most suitable response to that region's special environmental and traditional requirements. In the southern part of the state, the style is preeminently associated with the work of Charles Sumner Greene and Henry Mather Greene, whose background and training exemplify the familiar pattern of eastern architectural immigration. In 1893, when the Greene brothers were in their early twenties, they moved to Pasadena, where their parents had recently settled for health reasons. Once established in California, the Greenes worked for ten years through various revival vocabularies without producing anything of great originality or distinction. Then, rather suddenly, their work began to manifest a decidedly personal and regional stamp. This development seems to have resulted from a jointly shared passion for oriental forms and techniques sharpened by visits to the Japanese Village at the California Mid-Winter Exposition in San Francisco in 1894, and from Charles Greene's encounter in England with the Arts and Crafts Movement. Although less easily analyzed but ultimately of greatest importance, both brothers also appreciated their adopted land and its building traditions.

This creative phase began in 1903 with the house designed for Arturo Bandini, a descendant of an influential provincial family, that combined for the first time the central courtyard plan inherent in California's Hispanic tradition with the New Englanders' board-and-batten and shingle construction. To accentuate the importance of the physical environment, the Greene brothers constructed foundations, chimneys, and fireplaces of granite boulders taken from the neighboring arroyo. The Bandini House, demolished in 1961, was the first of the Greene and Greene bungalows. In light of its importance in popularizing what became a southern California vernacular, this house must be accounted as one of the Greenes's most significant designs.

It took several years of experimentation before they developed a compacted version of the Bandini prototype, of which the Neill House (Plate 14) is a well-known surviving example. Built originally for speculation, the house was extensively altered on the exterior by the architects in 1906. It is this revision that makes the Neill House so convincing a statement in the subsequent development of the California bungalow, embodying as it does almost every characteristic of the vernacular: horizontality, vigorous timbered expression, multiple roof overhangs, low but prominent entrance porch, clinker bricks, boulders placed decoratively into foundations, and because the automobile was crucial to the bungalow culture, a pergola-overhung driveway.

Modest dwellings such as the Neill House—and not the splendidly sited and superbly crafted "ultimate bungalows" designed by the Greenes for wintering millionaires—are important in the development of an American architecture relevant to the southern California "lifestyle." The Greenes did not invent the bungalow, nor indeed any aspect of its western form. However, as the designers of more than 150 bungalows, their work was crucial in the evolution of what must be accounted among the most significant architectural developments in California in the first quarter of the twentieth century. The Greenes gave to the West what their admirer and propagandist, Gustav Stickley of the *Craftsman* magazine, called "Houses for Indoor Comfort and Outdoor Living." The fact that the Greene brothers disapproved of the eventual development of the mass bungalow vernacular under speculative builders, who espoused only their forms and debased the quality of materials and workmanship that made their houses so celebrated (and expensive), did not lessen their influence. The strength of the bungalow movement is that it was based upon the best architectural designs, no matter what the ultimate sacrifice in quality. Like the Queen-Anne Eastlake urban row vernacular of a half-century earlier, the bungalow provided efficiently planned, well-lighted, and attractive housing to the large numbers of people of modest means who came to California in answer to the call of a good life in a sunny land.

The same sunny climate and the Mediterranean quality of the California coastal area helped determine the architectural character of another regional building

14. Neill House, Pasadena, 1903–1906. Greene and Greene, architects. Randall L. Makinson, *Greene & Greene: Architecture as a Fine Art* (Salt Lake and Santa Barbara: Peregrine Smith, Inc., 1977), p. 140. Courtesy of Peregrine Smith, Inc.

scheme which also originated with an eastern architect who had been one of the innovators of the Shingle Style. This was the influential plan for Stanford University originally conceived in the office of Henry Hobson Richardson, who was admired among his contemporaries for his personal version of the round arch style employed by early Christian builders in southern France and Spain. Known in architectural terminology as Richardsonian Romanesque (Plate 15), it was characterized by bold and plain surfaces of rough-cut stone and sparse and strongly incised ornament which Richardson felt best served the building requirements of the aggressive and powerful commercial society that he, a southerner, saw as the ultimate economic consequences of northern victory in the Civil War. Richardson's massive and forceful statements in rock-faced granite and cut sandstone, such as the Marshall Field Wholesale Store (1885–1887) in Chicago, were widely imitated throughout the nation in the last decades of the nineteenth century. Few of the California imitators, however, could master Richardson's style, and the regional results were designated by San Francisco's classicist Willis Polk as a "Titanic inebriation." There are, nevertheless, some worthy survivors within the Bay Area; the most notable are the original buildings of Leland Stanford, Jr. University (Plate 15), designed and executed between 1887 and 1891.

When Leland and Jane Stanford decided in 1885 they would build a university on their Palo Alto estate as a memorial to their only son who had died in Italy the previous year, they announced it must have "an architecture distinctly Californian in character."[3] The "Californian" elements particularly desired by the Stanfords were red tile roofs, courtyards, and long, deeply shaded arcades. The immediate sources for the building elements favored by the Stanfords were the ruined Franciscan missions, whose possibilities for a regional architecture were only just then being discovered by Willis Polk and a few eastern friends such as John Galen Howard. Themselves recognizing that the California missions and Richardsonian Romanesque shared a common architectural tradition, and impressed by both the fame and the monumentality of Richardson's work, the Stanfords turned to him for the material realization of their all-absorbing passion to create a great university. It appeared to have been a choice favored by precedent: Richardson had already produced some of the greatest American architecture of the nineteenth century through collaboration with clients—the railroad builder, Oakes Ames and the merchant, Marshall Field—similar in dominance and decision to Leland Stanford.

15. Stanford University, Palo Alto, 1887–1891. Shepley, Rutan and Coolidge, architects. Courtesy of the Bancroft Library.

Richardson died before he could become involved in the Palo Alto project and the work was turned over to his successor firm, Shepley, Rutan and Coolidge, and the landscape architect Frederick Law Olmsted. The initial plan was thoughtfully designated by Leland Stanford as "an adaptation of the adobe building of California, with some higher form of architecture."[4] Although the dominant features of the original buildings were absolutely based upon specific Richardsonian sources, the general spirit of the project, and particularly its plan and landscape design, reflected conditions that Stanford held to be "distinctly Californian in character," even the use of Hispanic terminology for dormitory and street names. As Karen Weitze has observed, Stanford University was the first "major design that deliberately drew upon the missions," and as such "marked a turning point in the architectural development of late nineteenth-century California."[5]

The Richardson Romanesque buildings that comprised the nucleus of Stanford University can be perceived as containing many of the elements that sustained the Mission Revival. The chief artifact was the Franciscan mission, a colonial variant of the Romanesque monasteries of Spain whose own origin lay in the ancient Mediterranean world. The comparison between southern California—the principal arena of the mission legend—and the Mediterranean littoral has always been noted, and not only because of similarity in climate and topography but also because of the presence of a pastoral life and a citrus culture in California's early economy. The legend was largely developed by easterners, especially New Englanders, who were also strongly oriented to Europe and the Mediterranean region. The fact that Stanford University, the first important transitional monument of the Mission Revival, was designed by a Boston firm, only one of whose members had seen a mission, also supports the familiar theme of cultural colonialism.

As well as exhibiting the transference of European building forms to America, the Mission Style is properly part of a national movement of historical discovery that began with the Philadelphia Centennial of 1876. Just as Northeasterners sought to return, stylistically at least, to the picturesque wood structures of their colonial past—hence the Shingle Style soon to flourish on the West Coast—so Californians looked to the ruins of the Franciscan missions as a means for regional identity. The new style, as one of them exclaimed, caught their imagination: "Give me neither Romanesque nor Gothic; much less Italian Renaissance, and least of all English colonial—this is California—give me Mission."[6] The missions became, through literary, artistic, preservationist, and promotional agencies, the major source in California's search for its "mythic" past.

Like the revival of medievalism in England almost a century earlier, the Mission Style began as a literary movement. One of its earliest and most celebrated progenitors was Helen Hunt Jackson, whose popular novel *Ramona* (1884) was preceded by pilgrimages to nearly every mission from San Diego to Sonoma. This physical contact with the picturesque ruins of Franciscan building in California gave probability to an otherwise presumed and sentimental portrayal of an idyllic and moral society that vanished with the Gold Rush. The illustrator of *Ramona,* the Canadian artist Henry Sandham, composed his evocative drawings from field sketches in company with Helen Hunt Jackson. These drawings, together with the paintings of the Scotsman William Keith and the Englishman Edward Deakin, were almost as essential as Jackson's prose in conveying to the now largely Anglo-Saxon urban Californians the sense of the mission presence upon which the architectural revival was based. The missions supplied not only the most notable, but also almost the only material remnant upon which legend could be constructed. In a remarkable replay of England's Gothic Revival, the builders of California's expanding commercial society seized upon the architecture of a monastic and pastoral life as the form for the hotels, railroad stations, business blocks, country houses, suburban dwellings, and bungalows of a secular and rapidly urbanizing state.

Jackson, a New Englander, wrote the first novel about southern California. Another New Englander, the Harvard-educated Charles Fletcher Lummis, was the first to realize the material, as opposed to the moral and artistic, values of the movement when he wrote that the missions "are worth more money, are a greater asset to Southern California, than our oil, our oranges, or even our climate."[7] Lummis's major propaganda organ was the *Land of Sunshine,* and his editorial efforts employed the same promotional devices used in the concurrent health and real estate booms.

Lummis's message for architecture was that in California's Hispanic past lay not only a mine of literary and artistic imagery but also a design solution to the state's rapidly expanding need for commercial, institutional, and residential construction. He presumed that the mission would supply the model for the architecture of "modern" California and he was the first to suggest stucco on metal lath and concrete as the new technologies' substitute for traditional masonry construction. Lummis was also outstanding as a preservationist, founding, in 1894, the Landmarks Club, whose chief purpose was the restoration of the ruined mission buildings. He believed that the restoration of the missions—displaying them as the original complex rather than the isolated and ruined component—would reveal the true presence behind the legend and remind Californians that if "Plymouth Rock was a state of mind, so [too] were the California missions."[8]

Like all states of mind, the California mission version, relating as it did to life juxtaposed to land and sun and distant sea, had many usages. Its promotional value in the field of tourism was recognized from the beginning of its dissemination. One of the most attractive results of the parallel efforts to project nationally a regional identity, based upon Hispanic imagery and the stimulation of tourism, was the widespread construction of Mission Revival railway stations throughout California in the late 1890s and early 1900s. As the visitor's first direct encounter with the land was usually through the railroad passenger depot, promoters of the idea felt that the design of these structures should contain the strongest possible reference to the mission, which was being used as the state's richest architectural symbol. It was fortunate that the linear requirements of the passenger depot, although naturally without Franciscan precedent, fitted more harmoniously to the long line of tile-roofed arcades and terraced bell towers than most contemporary building programs. The mission imagery was so successfully exploitated in California railroad depot construction that it spread subsequently to all parts of the Southwest which shared a mission past and a tourist present.

The extant Southern Pacific Depot in Burlingame (Plate 16) was begun late in 1893, the year in which the Mission Revival achieved national recognition with the California Building at the World's Columbian Exposition in Chicago. The California Building was the first large-scale monument to the Mission Revival, and with its random borrowing of design elements from Mission, Moorish, and Richardsonian Romanesque sources and its construction in rough stucco over lath in imitation of adobe, embodied both the chief characteristics and dichotomies of the Mission Style. The architect of this influential building, A. Page Brown, had moved his office from New York to San Francisco four years earlier with the avowed intention of designing for the leaders of that metropolis such Eastern refinements as the Shingle Style house and the country club community.

The commission for the railroad depot in Burlingame was inevitably given to Brown, who was one of the original developers of the suburban community that the depot was to serve. At this time, however, Brown's architectural firm was completely immersed in the plans and the construction of a far more important railroad passenger terminal, the Ferry Building at the foot of Market Street in San Francisco. Brown turned over this smaller depot commission to George Howard

16. Southern Pacific Depot, Burlingame, 1893–94. Howard and Mathison, architects. Courtesy of the San Mateo County Historical Association.

and Joachim Mathisen who were, like himself, engaged in the development of Burlingame as a suburban park centered around a country club that included a race track and a polo field.

Mathisen was a European-trained engineer whose California career began in the office of A. Page Brown; Howard, sometimes partner of Bernard Maybeck, was the son of the owner of the original San Mateo Rancho upon which the station stands, and the designer of a number of houses in the vicinity of the country club. The depot design necessarily reflected their friend and mentor's recent and celebrated California State Building with its broad arcades, tile roof, quatrefoil window in a scalloped gable, and simulated masonry construction. More original are the terraced roof, square tower, and apparently for the first time, the incorporation of chimneys into a mission design—subsequently a much-used solution. Even more unusual, indeed perhaps unique, the roof tiles of the Burlingame station were handmade three-quarters of a century earlier by Indians from Mission San Antonio de Padua and San Mateo Assistencia and purchased by Howard from these ruined Franciscan establishments expressedly for the Burlingame station.

One of the ironies of the Mission Revival was its enthusiastic acceptance by both American adherents of the Arts and Craft Movement and regional promoters of modern techniques exemplified by the use of Portland cement in place of adobe. It was, in fact, by fusing the seemingly disparate interests of these groups that Irving Gill created the most distinguished of the Mission Style buildings. Gill, like so many of the contemporary architects, builders, and artisans who worked within this stylistic movement, came to southern California during the health boom. Settling in San Diego in 1893, he began an architectural practice preceded by a three-year apprenticeship in the Chicago office of Louis Sullivan. As a draftsman in this office, Gill worked, along with Frank Lloyd Wright, on the design for the Transportation Building for the World's Columbian Exposition. It was also for this exposition that A. Page Brown designed the California Building that first brought the Mission Revival to national attention. But it was Sullivan's dazzling structure, rather than the San Francisco architect's, that had a powerful and immediate influence upon Gill's work in California. Not only were the circular pavilions and famous "Golden Door" of the Transportation Building incorporated in some of his earliest San Diego designs, but its long line of deeply recessed arches prepared Gill for ultimate acceptance of the Franciscan mission as the basis for an architecture indigenous to California.

It took Gill, however, more than a decade to shake off his eastern thinking and training and respond creatively to the California environment. Writing long after-wards in the *Craftsman,* he described the then unspoiled southern coastal areas as "lovely little hills and canyons waiting to hold the record of this generation's history, ideals, imagination, sense of romance and honesty." Equally crucial in the development of a truly California architecture was Gill's slowly dawning appre-ciation of the ruined Franciscan missions. In the same article he wrote that their "long, low lines, graceful arcades, tile roofs, bell towers, arched doorways, and walled gardens [were] a most expressive medium of retaining tradition, history and romance.'"9 In the land, and in the oldest forms the Europeans had laid upon it, Gill found the sources for a regional architecture appropriate to southern California's physical environment, its colonial past, and the most recent structural innovations within the building trade.

The simplicity of the adobe builders appealed powerfully to Gill's "passion for elimination." He abandoned, in time, his eastern-learned wood and brick tech-niques for a system of reinforced concrete and hollow-tile construction finished with smooth concrete laid flush with roof and casings and wholly unadorned. The construction process was also simplified by his use of the tilt-slab method by which walls were fully laid upon a tilted platform and, when the concrete hard-ened, slowly raised into place. Sounding the call for architectural simplification in both material and design, Gill proclaimed a return to the earliest and most enduring components of design: the straight line, the arch, the cube, and the circle. The effect of this command is beautifully evident in the buildings Gill created for the Bishop's School (1909–1916) and Women's Club (1913) in La Jolla, and the Lewis Court in Sierra Madre (Plate 17). In these three projects, Gill was able to place the buildings in the physical environment—the open California landscape of neighboring sea and distant mountain—that he understood essential to the "romance and honesty" of a revival of the Franciscan mission architecture. In his creed of elimination and simplicity, Gill perceived how poorly the Mission Style conformed to crowded and artificial urban sites.

The Lewis Court (1910) was Gill's favorite project. As originally conceived and built, the twelve "workingmen's cottages" covered less than thirty percent of the site—a large square at the foot of the San Gabrial Mountains at an elevation of 840 feet. The sense of openness that Gill so personally identified with the south-ern California landscape was realized to a maximum degree in the modest con-fines of Lewis Court: each bungalow contained a loggia and a small private garden which, in turn, opened onto a central area treated as a common.

17. Lewis Court, Sierra Madre, 1910. Irving Gill, architect. Courtesy of the Architectural Drawing Collection, University Art Museum, Santa Barbara.

Gill's careful concern for the design and the environment of these "working-men's cottages" was an outstanding architectural expression of the Progressive movement in California politics which actually reached its climax of influence in Los Angeles the year the Lewis Court was completed. Many of the leaders of the Progressive movement in southern California were, like their principal architects, professionally trained easterners and midwesterners who had come because of health problems and entered one phase or another of the real estate and building trade. And although the Progressives' widest sweep was in the field of electoral reform and the suppression of vice, they worked to bring such amenities as light and fresh air and gardens into the living sphere of working-class families.

As well as fitting into this general atmosphere of high-minded reform, the Lewis Court project epitomized Gill's design philosophy by presenting an exterior of white, wholly unadorned cubes joined together by arcades and rooted to the land through the means of stone walls, pergolas, and trailing vines. The interiors of each of the bungalows display their architect's "passion for elimination" with baseboards, casings and wainscots flush with the walls, the line between wall and floor slightly rounded to form one continuous piece, indented fireplaces and raised concrete hearths, and walls devoid of ornament painted a dull white. Subsequently, additional cottages were crowded into the open areas and Gill's original spatial concept was largely lost.

Irving Gill shares with the American craftsmen Charles and Henry Greene the distinction of giving southern California perhaps its finest domestic architecture in the first quarter of the twentieth century. In each case, they came west as well trained young men who only after many years of derivative practices were sufficiently inspired by the land and its earlier building traditions to formulate a style both beautiful and appropriate to the environment. Although the creation of a vernacular was not the intent of either the Greenes or Gill, their work was the basis for the distinctive California bungalow of the 1920s. But as others have pointed out, there is a significant difference between the Greenes' craftsmanship of complexity and Gill's craftsmanship of simplicity. The former is an architecture of detail, traditional in its wood techniques, and highly idiosyncratic; the latter is an architecture of mass achieved through a revolution in design and building process. In his use of hollow-block and concrete construction, plain walls and frameless windows, Gill returned California architecture to the cube-like dwellings of the adobe builders (Plate 3) and the straight line and arch of the Franciscan missionaries (Plate 2).

18. Hibernia Bank, San Francisco, 1892. Albert Pissis, architect. Photograph before enlargement in 1905 and rebuilding in 1907. Courtesy of the Bancroft Library.

VI

Architectural Maturity

During the first quarter of the twentieth century—the most fruitful period in the careers of Irving Gill and Charles and Henry Greene—the balance of power in California visibly shifted to the southland. Before this time, the preponderant influences in finance, politics, and culture radiated securely from the north. Starting from the time of statehood, this power was principally focused within the San Francisco Bay area and a hundred-mile radius that included Sacramento, San Jose, and Monterey. But the forces of change were already evident in the south by the turn of the century and became, by the end of the second decade of the twentieth century, the tidal wave that shaped what was to become an internationally recognized style of California living. Because these forces were largely those of the future, the shift in power was scarcely perceptible to the declining San Francisco bastion with its large foreign-born population and cultural colonialism. The new culture that developed from the dominance of the southland drew its character from American migrations and the more indigenous factors of automobiles, highways, and subdivisions.

One of the early indicators of the shift in power appeared in the census figures of 1920 which showed the population of southern California outstripping the north for the first time. The census of the previous decade had shown twice as many people living in the northern part of the state than in the southern. The change was spectacular. The increase in population represented both the momentum of the mass migration to southern California during the health and real estate booms and the eventual emergence of Los Angeles as one of the largest metropolitan areas in the nation with emphasis on agriculture, petroleum, shipping, motion picture production, hydroelectric power, and everything connected with an automobile-oriented society. By the first decade of the twentieth century, Los Angeles had more automobiles and highways than any comparable American city, and increasing dependence upon automotive transportation profoundly effected the life of the area. The automobile diffused the population, encouraged subdivision of abundant and accessible land, and promoted leisure and tourism by opening the areas of mountain, deserts, and beaches. Unrelenting advertising, few labor disputes, and even the San Francisco earthquake and fire of 1906—which diverted business, capital, and immigration to the south—contributed to the shift in power that became more pronounced with each succeeding decade. By the middle of the twentieth century, this explosive centrifugation had largely transformed historic California in all measurable categories.

The first architectural indication of this transformation was the development of a building culture dependent upon the automobile and the Mission aesthetic, which was represented at its best by Gill and the Greenes. But initially, the architectural movement evolving in southern California was limited primarily to the domestic field and the tourist industry's related need for hotels and railroad stations. Northern California, and particularly its historic center San Francisco, would continue architectural primacy for another generation. The basis for such superiority—despite a waning economic position—was the extraordinary quality and professionalism of a handful of graduates of the Ecole des Beaux-Arts. Founded under the auspices of Louis XIV in the mid-seventeenth century, the Ecole des Beaux-Arts was the most prestigious training ground for American architects between the Civil War and World War I. Its importance rested not only upon the then unrivaled training and discipline implicit in so arduous and competitive a program but also in the model it offered for architectural education in the United States. Indeed, the emergence of an architectural profession as such in this country was as directly related to the dissemination of Ecole teaching methods as to the brilliance of its many American graduates.

The Ecole method was enthusiastically embraced in California for both design and professional reasons. In the polyglot society of California in the nineteenth century, the need was acute for a common design vocabulary and mutually acceptable standards of professional accreditation. An Ecole education satisfied both requirements. It also offered a coherent alternative to the exuberant but chaotic English-derived architecture of the 1870s and 1880s, a particularly attractive consideration for the rising young generation of California Progressives of the 1890s. Among these Progressive architects were Albert Pissis, the first Californian to be admitted to the Ecole, and John Galen Howard, a Californian by adoption who built the Berkeley campus of the University of California along the lines of the prize-winning plan of the Paris-trained Emile Bernard. At the same time, Howard patterned the curriculum of the School of Architecture from the one he knew as a student at the Ecole. Later, Arthur Brown, Jr., a native of Oakland, introduced the educational methods of his own Ecole patron, Victor Laloux, at the San Francisco Architectural Club. The New Yorker, Robert D. Farquhar, came west after studying six years in Paris and established himself as the leading proponent of the Ecole method in southern California.

The American Architectural Renaissance was a late-nineteenth and early-twentieth century reaction to the unrestrained picturesque quality of Victorian revivalism. It was the artistic component of the national search for order that followed the demise of sectional, agrarian America after the Civil War and the country's corresponding sudden and dizzy rise to world economic and political power. Particularly, the movement proclaimed the United States the inheritor of the European Renaissance and sought to impose upon building the Beaux-Arts method of rational planning and the collaboration of architect, sculptors, and painters in important civic projects. The origin of the movement is generally dated with the great monuments in the Renaissance style of the 1880s from the New York office of McKim, Mead and White, especially the Boston Public Library and the Villard House. These models imposed upon the entire nation a uniform standard of excellence that was not willful but ordered; not picturesque but rational; not individual but classical. Stylistically, the American Renaissance encompassed Beaux-Arts Classicism, the Second Renaissance Revival, and the Classical Revival.

Whether or not the Belgian Peter Portois was, as he claimed, the first graduate of the Ecole to practice in the United States, the cosmopolitan architecture he helped introduce into San Francisco in the 1850s supplied the setting in which Albert Pissis was reared. Of Pissis's early life, almost nothing is known other than he was brought to California from Mexico in 1858 at age six. His father was a Paris-educated physician and a leading member of San Francisco's large and influential French colony. The connection with Portois can only be conjectured; possibly it was crucial not only in giving the youthful Albert an example of the European-trained professional but also as a source of early architectural instruction. At any rate, Pissis was admitted to the Ecole in 1872 at age twenty and, four years later, completed his architectural education with the most distinguished record of any

American of his time. Pissis returned to San Francisco in 1877 with an academic knowledge of the fundamentals of construction and design perhaps more thorough than any contemporary American other than his Ecole compatriots Richard Morris Hunt, H. H. Richardson, and Charles McKim.

Beaux-Arts Classicism reached California in 1889 with Pissis's winning design for the Hibernia Bank of San Francisco (Plate 18). This was the first building on the Pacific Coast to achieve international acclamation and owed its success both to the foresight of the client and the ability of the architect. The bank directors, determined to have a building fully commensurate with their institution's position as the state's largest bank, deemed the project sufficiently important to organize a national competition. Equally significant was the condition that the building be a free-standing, independent structure unencumbered by the usual floors of speculative office space above the street-level banking facilities. Finally, the site selected was an important corner near the City Hall that offered two facades as opposed to the single one of most contemporary bank buildings. In both the competitive and programmatic requirements it was the ideal Ecole project and, not unnaturally, the prize went to the first Californian to master the Beaux-Arts method.[1]

The enormous enthusiasm, even reverence, that greeted Pissis's bank building can only be understood in the context of San Francisco's confused late Victorian streetscape. By the 1870s the restrained Italianate of the late Gold Era had given way to the most extravagant succession of stylistic references which, for all their picturesqueness, were jarring and specious. Then suddenly there appeared the beautifully ordered pale granite structure with seven bays on one facade and five on the other. These two facades were joined by a copper-domed rotunda. The Hibernia Bank gave Californians their first lesson in the Beaux-Arts method: a plan organized around interior spatial requirements and a facade that developed logically from such internal necessity. The result was a rational, spacious, and well lighted interior and an exterior that was, especially for the times, extremely austere and correct. Added to the overall architectural quality of the Hibernia Bank building was an attention to detail and craftsmanship absent in almost all contemporary California construction. Even the dependably cynical Willis Polk was cowed to near silence; he proclaimed it simply the most beautiful building in San Francisco.

The Hibernia Bank was followed by a noteworthy succession of commercial and public structures that popularized the academic movement as far north as

Eureka and south to San Diego. Some of these "splendid survivors," such as San Francisco's Emporium and Flood buildings (1896 and 1904), were designed by Pissis himself; others were the work of the dozen or more former Ecole students who were practicing in the Bay Area, Sacramento, and Los Angeles at the time of the 1906 earthquake and fire. Competing with the Ecole alumni was a growing number of equally distinguished designers who received their Beaux-Arts oriented instruction in the New York office of McKim, Mead and White, or in its West Coast counterpart, the San Francisco atelier of A. Page Brown. The most notable member of this group was Willis Polk, whose Hallidie Building (Plate 19) has been the subject of international attention since its construction in 1917–1918.

The Hallidie Building is historically foremost among California's commercial structures because of its long claim to be "The World's First Glass Front Building." This attribution may not be technically accurate, but Polk's Hallidie Building is the first major urban example of glass-curtain construction. Furthermore, none of the several earlier glass-fronted structures was without supporting columns or ribbons of masonry, as is the case with the Hallidie Building, whose all-glass facade is cantilevered three feet in front of its supporting reinforced concrete frame. Equally original is Polk's treatment of the pair of fire escapes as an integral part of the design rather than a grudging protrusion in compliance with a building code. These, and the four bands of late Victorian cast-iron decoration, create a fanciful contrast to the twentieth-century glass plane which reflects their reverse sides as well as the facade of neighboring buildings. The sense of fantasy invoked by Polk's masterpiece was heightened by the original blue and gold paint that proclaimed its builder-owners to be the Regents of the University of California.

At the time of the construction of the Hallidie Building, Willis Polk was among the state's most influential architects. He was certainly the most notorious, patterning his public life on the acerbic model of the painter Whistler and his private one on architect Stanford White. But Polk was more than a brilliant designer; he was California's preeminent example in the arts of the self-made man. Polk's basic professional education was acquired in a family of builder-contractors, and only much later as a draftsman in New York City was he somewhat irregularly admitted into the inner circle of the academic movement. When A. Page Brown moved his office to San Francisco in 1889, he asked Polk to join him, and although never a licensed architect, Polk was the dominant design force in the formative years of California's first great architectural office. Later, when the international firm of

19. Hallidie Building, San Francisco, 1917–1918. Willis Polk, architect. Photograph by Roy Flamm. Courtesy of the Bancroft Library.

D. H. Burnham and Company established an office in San Francisco, Willis Polk was named its head.

Daniel Burnham was the entrepreneurial half of the most distinguished Chicago office after Adler and Sullivan. Following the early death of his brilliant partner, John Wellborn Root, he turned increasingly to civic planning and by 1900 was the leader in the City Beautiful movement that dominated American urban design from the 1880s through the 1920s. In 1904, when Burnham was invited to prepare a plan for the "Improvement and Adornment of San Francisco," his office was already known for the old Chronical Building (1886–1889), the first iron and steel frame building in the West; the Mills Building (1890–1891), the city's earliest entirely steel-frame structure and California's finest example of Chicago School design; and the recent Merchant's Exchange Building designed by the company's San Francisco representative, Willis Polk. The latter, the prototype for California's great downtown office buildings in the quarter century following construction in 1904, proved far more influential than Polk's more famous but idiosyncratic Hallidie Building.

The City Beautiful movement in San Francisco was part of a broad coalition of Progressive businessmen, lawyers, editors, educators, and civic leaders formed to combat municipal political corruption. Many of the reformers were friends or clients of Willis Polk, and the appointment of his colleague-employer Daniel Burnham as San Francisco's master planner was not unnatural. Burnham's plan more than vindicated the choice. Combining the grandeur of Beaux-Arts planning with the latest concepts of transportation, sanitation, and preservation, the plan had as its core a civic center at the intersection of Market Street and Van Ness Avenue. These avenues were to be transformed into magnificent thoroughfares bisected by other great arteries running west to Golden Gate Park and the ocean and south to the Southern Pacific Railway Station. The hills would be beautified with parks, the shore line protected, and public facilities such as subways, hospitals, schools, and jails were to be constructed with an eye to beauty as well as utility. The plan was accepted late in 1905; six months later the earthquake struck and the resulting fire destroyed not only the original plan and models but all hope of implementation. As was the case with Sir Christopher Wren's plan for London in 1666, the economic arguments of the rapid reconstructionists carried the day.

But the enthusiasm generated by Burnham's plan could not be entirely checked. One positive result of the 1906 holocaust was the destruction of San Francisco's third city hall, a monument of architectural and political corruption in whose execution several design careers and six million dollars were swallowed up. Determined to salvage something of their City Beautiful hopes, a coalition of Progressive civic leaders and architects created the Civic Center and held a competition for the design of the new city hall (Plate 20). The competition, unlike the previous international one that produced the Hearst Plan for the University of California, was limited to San Franciscans. The winning design was from the office of Bakewell and Brown and established one of the partners, Arthur Brown, Jr., as the new leader on the West Coast of the American Renaissance.

Brown completed what has been praised as "the greatest architectural ensemble in America" when he counterpoised the city hall with two flanking buildings of identical facades—the War Memorial Opera House and the War Memorial Veteran's Building (both 1932)—separated by piers with monumental gates.[2] The grandeur and coherency of this plan makes the Van Ness Avenue axis of San Francisco's civic center the nation's outstanding example of the Beaux-Arts method and style. The only city in California that successfully emulated the San Francisco prototype was Pasadena, and there, again, the city hall (1925–1927) dominates a splendid axial composition with complementary auditorium (1925–1927) and library (1927). Pasadena's City Hall is also the work of Bakewell and Brown, who responded to the competition for a building suggestive of the climate and environment of the Mediterranean with a stunning pink Baroque structure encompassing a landscaped court with fountain.

Arthur Brown, Jr. was born in Oakland in 1874, the son of the Scottish-educated superintendent of bridge and building construction for the Southern Pacific Railroad. In the absence of an architectural school at the University of California until early in the twentieth century, Brown enrolled as an engineering student and, with seven other architecturally oriented collegians, studied design informally in the house of Bernard Maybeck, Ecole graduate and recently appointed instructor in drawing in the Civil Engineering College. Among Maybeck's first "class," all of whom went on to complete their training at the Beaux-Arts, were Brown's future sometime partner, the Kansas-born John Bakewell; the young Englishman Edward Bennett, later of Burnham's Chicago office and probably chief architect of the San Francisco plan; and the native San Franciscan Julia Morgan, America's most celebrated female architect, the first woman admitted to the Ecole, and designer of more than 500 buildings, including William Randolph Hearst's San Simeon (1919–1940). In Paris, Brown studied under Victor Laloux, one of the outstanding French architects of the time, and proved so promising that his patron tried to

20. City Hall, San Francisco, 1915. Bakewell and Brown, architects. Photograph by Chauncey A. Kirk.

induce him to take French citizenship in order to compete for the Grand Prix de Rome. Brown received his diploma in 1903, served a brief but important apprenticeship in Washington, D.C., and returned to San Francisco to establish a partnership with his Berkeley and Ecole compatriot John Bakewell. By the time of the 1912 San Francisco City Hall competition, the firm was well known for residential work, as architects for Stanford University's post-Richardsonian building, and the Berkeley City Hall (1908).

More than a hundred architects competed in the San Francisco City Hall project with its first prize of ten thousand dollars and a four million dollar building contract. The program called for a design that would make an architecturally symbolic statement as well as provide sufficient space for the many requirements of a modern municipal bureaucracy. Bakewell and Brown's winning design accomplished this by a dominating dome—the traditional American symbol of government—that also served to organize and illuminate the interior space. It has been said that the city hall "succeeds so far beyond most such 20th century efforts at Renaissance grandeur that it invited comparison with its models."[3] Essentially these are Jules Hardouin Mansart's dome of the Invalides (1679–1691) and the 1878 Grand Prix de Rome design for a cathedral by Brown's Ecole patron Victor Laloux. Accepted today as the nation's finest city hall, Bakewell and Brown's first masterpiece was viewed at the time of construction as the country's foremost symbol of the Progressive impulse toward political and architectural order.

The Beaux-Arts tradition that began regionally with Pissis's Hibernia Bank culminated in San Francisco's civic center and the Panama Pacific International Exposition of 1915. The Exposition's ostensible purpose was to celebrate the completion of the Panama Canal. In fact, there were also more pragmatic intentions: to announce the emergence of San Francisco as the great international port of a new Pacific empire, to signal the city's spectacular recovery from the devastating earthquake and fire of a decade earlier, and to demonstrate that the Architectural Renaissance begun in the Midwest with the Chicago Columbian Exposition had reached its artistic apogee on the western edge of the continent. None of these intentions was more successfully realized than the latter, especially as evidence in Bernard Maybeck's Palace of Fine Arts (Plate 21), perhaps the most beautiful and evocative monument raised in America to the spirit of fantasy and promotion that is the essence of the modern world's fair.

The genesis of the Palace of Fine Arts was a series of happenstances. Although known locally at the time for his pioneering classes in architecture at the Uni-

21. Palace of Fine Arts, San Francisco, 1915. Bernard Maybeck, architect. Photograph by Roy Flamm. Courtesy of the Bancroft Library.

versity of California, for his association with the Hearst Plan for the Berkeley campus, as the architect of a number of small but admired Bay Area houses, and a single masterpiece (Berkeley's First Church of Christ, Scientist 1910), Maybeck was not assigned any part in the planning of the exposition. His office was closed at the time for lack of work, and he was temporarily employed as a draftsman by his old friend Willis Polk. Polk and Maybeck had met as itinerant young designers in Kansas City twenty-five years earlier and shortly after Maybeck had returned from Paris. At Polk's prompting and the promise of work in A. Page Brown's office, Maybeck joined his friend in San Francisco late in 1890. But in the intervening decades Maybeck did not share in Polk's professional and social success, which culminated in his appointment as supervising architect of the Panama Pacific International Exposition. Inevitably, Polk was assigned the most important exposition project: the Palace of Fine Arts to be sited at the western terminus of three great courts that paralleled the Bay in what is now San Francisco's Marina district. The design that came out of Polk's office was received with extravagant praise by the Architectural Commission, which was composed of distinguished eastern architects and firms, including McKim, Mead and White. The conception and rendering were Maybeck's, and Polk, with his noted generosity, immediately proclaimed its authorship, renounced the commission, and insisted that it be given exclusively to Maybeck.

The universal appeal of the Palace of Fine Arts lay in the mood the architect evoked in the imagination of the fairgoer. The mood, as Maybeck explained in a little keepsake dedicated to Willis Polk, was one of sadness softened by beauty. The element of sadness related to the passing of all human efforts; the serious note reflected a world then at war. Architecture, Maybeck asserted, was a conveyor of ideas and sentiments; the crucial step in the design process is to "examine a historic form and see whether the effect it produced on your mind matches the feeling you are trying to portray."[4] This is a statement of the Beaux-Arts principle that design should be evolutionary, basing itself upon great monuments of the past interpreted in terms of contemporary programs. For Maybeck the mood he sought was Rome as seen in the eighteenth-century engravings of Piranesi, in which crumbling monuments are portrayed overgrown with trees and vegetation. Drawing upon the expressionistic genius first evident in the Berkeley Christian Science Church, he created an octagonal rotunda in orange, pink, and ocher backed with a peristyle that curved to the line of the lagoon. The whole structure was planted with trees, shrubs, and vines to convey the sense of an antique ruin.

OLD FORMS ON A NEW LAND

Whether seen in brilliant sunlight against the blue California sky or floodlighted on a foggy evening, Maybeck's enchantment was irresitible. And in defiance of the planned impermanence and purposefully contrived mood of sad transience that the architect had so skillfully engendered, a movement was launched by Willis Polk to save the Palace of Fine Arts even before the Exposition ended. The problem was that although the structure was sound, the walls and ornaments were constructed of plaster of Paris and hemp fiber. For almost half a century the monument crumbled and the landscaping around the lagoon grew wild and lush—a process Maybeck viewed with delight; after all, he had conceived of it as a ruin. Finally, beginning in 1962 and at a cost of six million dolars, the Palace of Fine Arts was rebuilt with some modifications in reinforced concrete. The success of the reconstruction is a matter of debate. Some, offended by the hardness of the material and rawness of color, recall with regret Maybeck's own solution that the monument be permitted to decay and then be replaced with a redwood grove.

The Panama Pacific Exposition and the San Francisco Civic Center marked the apogee of the California phase of the American Renaissance. But even after the onset of the Great Depression, the classical language disseminated from the Ecole des Beaux-Arts continued to dominate the major building circles centered in San Francisco and Los Angeles. The stylistic manifestation that the Beaux-Arts tradition assumed during its final phase is known variously as Art Deco, Moderne, and Modernistic. The general nature of the style is best revealed by the term Art Deco, an abbreviation of Exposition des Arts Décoratifs, the Paris design fair of 1925 that promoted not only traditional artistic artifacts but new industrial materials such as aluminum. The style came to be largely defined by shape and ornament. Commercial structures, for example, might be called Zigzag Modern and the numerous schools, libraries, and post offices constructed by the Public Works Administration were called Classical Moderne. And though its immediate sources were such contemporary ones as the movies, jazz, and cubism, the style as structure was based upon long accepted Beaux-Arts ideas of planning, composition, and urbanism. This integration of the European past and the American present is beautifully evident in the Los Angeles Public Library (Plate 22), designed by Bertram Goodhue in 1922 and completed in 1926, two years after his death by Carleton Monroe Winslow.

Unlike the usual California-born or Beaux-Arts bred diplomist, whose French training was hardly altered by New World environmental or historical factors,

22. Public Library, Los Angeles, 1922–1926. Bertram B. Goodhue and Carleton M. Winslow, architects. Courtesy of the Architectural Drawing Collection, University Art Museum, Santa Barbara.

Goodhue and Winslow responded to western regional conditions with an intensity and originality akin to that of Irving Gill. Goodhue and Winslow were New Englanders with roots going back to the seventeenth century. They shared an appreciation of both North and South American building traditions that was absent in Albert Pissis and Arthur Brown, Jr., both of whom were children of European immigrants and remained all their lives culturally oriented to France. Pissis and Brown were also professionally active in San Francisco, which was always drawn to the Old World, while Goodhue and Winslow worked in the Los Angeles area, which represented the final wave of successive continental migrations.

Carleton Winslow studied in Paris at the same time as Brown, but Goodhue was not Ecole-trained. He imbibed the reigning classicism through his mentor and long-time partner, Ralph Adams Cram. In his thinking and practice, Goodhue was ambivalent regarding the Beaux-Arts; he accepted its authority and discipline, but retained a strong attachment to medieval and Hispanic sources. His sense of architecture was global rather than European. In Goodhue's first California commission, the widely acclaimed house and gardens for J. Waldron Gillespie in Montecito in 1906, Goodhue traveled to Persia as well as to the Mediterranean for design inspiration. Nine years later, when he was appointed architect for the Panama-California Exposition in San Diego, he resisted the academic French style that prevailed in the more famous San Francisco exposition of the same year. Instead, Goodhue struck out boldly in the direction of the colonial origins of southern California by designing the 1915 San Diego Exposition in the Spanish and Mexican Churrigueresque style.

The exotic Churriguresque was not, however, the style he utilized in his most important California commission, the Los Angeles Public Library, which was completed about a decade after the San Diego exposition and which was judged southern California's "greatest single architectural composition."[5] This project reflects Goodhue's unique ability to suggest, by architectural abstraction, the Mediterranean and Near Eastern sources which he felt were most appropriate to the California environment, as well as his acceptance of the spatial discipline of classicism. The stripped-down classicism of the library design is representative of much Moderne public building of the 1920s. So too are the library's orderly but asymmetrical facades which, in correct Beaux-Arts fashion, suggest internal function: a series of well-lighted reading rooms surrounding a central book stack of seven levels terminating in a highly colored mosaic-crowned pyramidal roof. The interior space conforms to the logical, axial planning that two generations of Paris-trained architects had imposed upon American building standards. The modernity evident in the term Moderne is emphasized structurally through the use of reinforced concrete and industrial sash windows. Finally, the Beaux-Arts insistence that architecture be joined to all the fine arts is fulfilled by an ambitious sculptural program defined as "Light," a series of allegorical paintings depicting the four great eras of California history, and extensive landscaping reflecting Goodhue's favored Mediterranean sources.

It was from these Mediterranean sources and their regional adaptations in the Americas that Goodhue launched the Spanish Colonial Revival with his design for the San Diego Fair in 1915. In its origins, the movement enkindled through the enthusiasm of a New England convert was similar to the earlier Mission Revival of which it was both part and extension. Aside from a shared New England patrimony, there were marked differences between the two phases of California's Mediterranean Revival. The Spanish Colonial was not primarily a literary-inspired and tourist-oriented style; nor was it overlaid with the moralistic and reforming connotations of the Mission movement. Furthermore, no one claimed that California had a truly Spanish past, whereas it had at least a visible mission presence. Goodhue, and such other Spanish Colonial Revivalists as Myron Hunt and Elmer Gray, likened only California's land and climate to the Mediterranean region. The environmental factors of the Spanish Colonial phase were clearly valid. And of great practical importance, the sources for the Spanish Colonial Revival afforded far more possibilities for contemporary adaptation to a wide range of public and domestic architecture than had the necessarily limited building vocabulary of the Franciscans in California.

The architectural climate of the Spanish Colonial Revival was also much changed from that prevailing in the period of the Mission Style. For even though the motivation of both phases of the larger Mediterranean movement was the same—to discover and promote a distinctive California architectural identity—the Spanish Colonialists represented the new school of architects who were trained in the Beaux-Arts to use specific historical references rather than the loose adaptations that characterized much of the Mission work. The new eclecticism was fostered by European study and travel as well as a great increase in the publication of architectural sources, primarily by means of photography. Goodhue was not unusual among the Spanish Revivalists in publishing a pictorial record of his Mexican travels. His talented colleague, Richard Requa, published, in 1929, a book whose title clearly explained its purpose: *Old World Inspiration for American*

23. County Courthouse, Santa Barbara, 1929. William Mooser Company, architects. Photograph by Greg Alcorn.

Architecture. The growing preservation movement, whose first major regional objective was the reconstruction of the California missions in the early twentieth century, introduced architects to historical archaeology and brought with it a greatly increased awareness of stylistic accuracy. In general, however, the Californians continued to be freer in their use of historical sources than was the case with contemporary American Colonial and Tudor Revivalists in the eastern states.

In the matter of historical selectivity, Goodhue led the way, learning early in his California residence that the flamboyant Churrigueresque style he introduced with the San Diego Exposition was unsuitable for most twentieth-century building. Crucial in this discovery was his growing admiration of Irving Gill's austere work, which he pronounced among the "most thoughtful" being done in California. As the Los Angeles Public Library shows, Goodhue's subsequent designs reflected a dramatic departure from the florid late Baroque of his earlier Spanish and Spanish American prototypes. This tendency toward simplification, indeed almost abstraction, became a major stylistic distinction of the Spanish Colonial Revival and is best seen in the work of George Washington Smith, an easterner who studied architecture at Harvard University and painting in Paris. Smith took as his models the haciendas and farmhouses of Andalusia, and his gleaming white cubes and rectangles with bare stretches of plastered walls and low roofs of red tile created a deservedly admired Santa Barbara vernacular.

The Santa Barbara County Court House (Plate 23), "the grandest Spanish Colonial Revival structure ever built,"[6] is principally the work of the San Francisco firm of William Mooser and Company—the state's oldest architectural office, founded in 1854 by a young Swiss immigrant. At the time of the construction of the Court House in 1929, the firm was headed by William Mooser, Jr., and William Mooser III. The latter was a graduate of the Ecole and a seventeen-year resident of France and Spain. Collaborating with the Moosers was Joseph Plunkett of the Santa Barbara architectural firm of Edwards and Plunkett, authors of the nearby Fox Arlington Theatre (1929), another great monument of the Spanish Colonial Revival. The result is a beautifully integrated structure (actually three separate buildings including a five-story jail) sensitively related to a vast sunken garden of stone terraces and half-century old pines, palms, and redwoods. The Court House is equally impressive from every vantage point and is rich in wit, fantasy, and surprises. It is a treasure house of architectural and decorative devices— archways, towers, and loggias; tiled walls, vaults, and floors; wrought-iron grills, balconies, and lanterns—in which nothing is repeated or exactly alike. The splendid integration of all branches of the fine arts testifies to the Beaux-Arts training of William Mooser III and relates the Santa Barbara Court House to Goodhue's slightly earlier Los Angeles Public Library.

At the same time, in the northern part of the state, there was a similar search for a distinctive regional architecture. Its source was not in the Mediterranean confluence but the immanent Anglo-Hispanic building of Provincial and Gold Rush California. The first, and indeed definitive, statement was the Santa Cruz farmhouse (Plate 24) designed in 1926 by William Wilson Wurster for the family of the University of California regent, Warren Gregory. With its redwood frame, shingled roof, exterior shutters, and linear system of circulation by doors opening on to a porch or terrace, the Gregory Farmhouse is the transitional structure between the Hispanic and Yankee builders of the 1830s and 1840s and the postwar tract "ranch house" that is the single most influential architecture yet to come out of California.

Wurster was born in the farming community of Stockton in 1895 and was, after Arthur Brown, Jr., the first native Californian to achieve an international architectural reputation. Like Brown, his formal professional training was entirely within the tradition of the Beaux-Arts. He studied architecture under John Galen Howard at Berkeley, apprenticed in the San Francisco office of the Ecole-trained John Reid, traveled in Europe for a year sketching and making measured drawings of historic monuments, and in 1923 entered the prestigious New York office of Delano and Aldrich, both of whose senior partners were Beaux-Arts graduates. The close personal relationship that developed between Chester Holmes Aldrich and Wurster lasted until the older man's death in 1960, and is thought to be one of the most important influences upon the Californian's professional life. In 1926, Wurster opened a San Francisco office and his first major commission was the Gregory Farmhouse.

Wurster's attitude toward site and client, as well as his role as educator, are crucial to understanding the enormous influence he exerted upon domestic architecture both in California and the nation for almost half a century. First, he maintained, the site must be accepted totally. It is said that immediately upon seeing the oak-studded, rolling coastal foothills upon which the Gregory's proposed to build, Wurster sketched the design from which scarcely any deviation was made in construction. But concurrent with the acceptance of the building site must be the appreciation and the advancement of the client's needs. The particular object of the California client, he wrote in 1949 while serving as Dean of

24. Gregory Farmhouse, Santa Cruz, 1926–1927. William Wilson Wurster, architect. Photograph by Roger Sturtevant. Courtesy of the Oakland Museum.

Architecture and Planning at Massachusetts Institute of Technology, is for "personally controlled" out-of-door living space. Seven years later, Wurster returned to California as Dean of the School of Architecture at Berkeley and enunciated his definitive rule of design: "architecture is for life and for pleasure and for work and for people . . . the picture frame and not the picture."[7]

In an article entitled "California Architecture for Living" in the April 1954 issue of *California Monthly,* Wurster included photographs of two historic buildings that suggested the direct, unstudied approach he thought appropriate to California: the Monterey Style Vallejo Adobe near Petaluma, distinguished for its "sense of fitness to site and purpose," and the William Downie House in Downieville, a two-story, straightforward clapboard house with large paired double-hung windows that "might fit with ease into almost any part of New England."[8] Wurster's integration of the potentials or the demands of the site with the needs of the client, coupled with an appreciation of Anglo-Hispanic building traditions, were the basis for a distinguished western architecture that was described in the citation accompanying the presentation in 1969 of the Gold Medal of the American Institute of Architects as "undogmatic, non-doctrinaire, forthright in its response to local and regional conditions."[9]

Between the construction of the Gregory Farmhouse and the beginning of the Great Depression, Wurster designed a few large handsome houses reflecting the Regency style favored by his mentors, Delano and Aldrich. After 1929, however, the field of California's domestic architecture was restricted largely to the design of small houses generally of inexpensive redwood construction. Wurster's California background and unusual sensitivity to the buildings of an earlier and even more materially impoverished period prepared him to accept these seeming limitations and out of them create an appropriate and appealing style. Between 1927 and 1942, he designed over two hundred houses and became the leader in the development of a regional domestic architecture that Frank Lloyd Wright labeled with some affection, the "shack style."[10] These were modest houses, usually one story in height with either board-and-batten or fitted-board construction of unpainted redwood and large windows and glass doors opening on to small courts or terraces. The simple elegance and individualism evident in these relatively inexpensive houses were partly the result of economies achieved by a generally applied "Wurster formula" that included double-hung windows, native materials such as redwood, the absence or simplification of door and window frames, and whenever possible, the elimination of floor level changes. But for all their modesty, the houses were individual and satisfying expressions of the needs of their time, their site, and their clients. The compatible Gregory prototype was never abandoned; economy was joined with quality and simplicity with refinement.

At the same time that William Wilson Wurster was leading northern Californians to the discovery of an architecture representative both of their Anglo-Hispanic past and the requirements of Depression Age economics and technology, the Austrian immigrant Richard J. Neutra was acquainting southern Californians with the first phase of the International Style as learned from his mentor, the austere modernist, Adolf Loos. The vehicle was the highly publicized Lovell House (Plate 25), constructed in the Hollywood Hills in 1929 and described by Rayner Banham as "a purely European vision of Machine Age architecture."[11] The completely steel frame of the Lovell House, the first to be used in American residential construction, was planted in a heavy ferroconcrete foundation and supported such novel prefabricated elements as clamp-on casement windows, steel and concrete panels, and Model A Ford headlights for interior illumination. Neutra not only designed the house and much of its furniture, but also acted as his own general contractor and landscape architect. The Lovell House, contemporaneously the most famous "modern" residence in California, earned for its architect immediate world recognition.

The International Style which the Lovell House characterizes is the culmination of a process toward architectural Modernism that gained significant impetus more than a century ago with the Arts and Crafts Movement in England. Combining veneration for the vanishing arts and crafts and a rejection of the emerging machine-age industry, the movement spread westward to America where, in California, the Greene brothers of Pasadena were among its most celebrated practitioners. But what the movers of the Arts and Crafts could not accept—the machine, became in the end the basis for a "modern" architecture that was significantly shaped by such New World influences as American industrial design, the Chicago School of Louis Sullivan, and the open plan of Frank Lloyd Wright. In fact, Wright is generally credited with propagating architectural modernism in southern California. Between 1917 and 1924, he designed five houses for the environs of Los Angeles; one of them, the massive Mayan pre-Columbian style Ennis House (1924), is within a long stone's throw of the Lovell House.

Richard Neutra discovered the early work of Frank Lloyd Wright in the Wasmuth folios published in Berlin in 1910–1911, and they served as a major influence

25. Lovell House, Los Angeles, 1927–1929. Richard Neutra, architect. Photograph by Julius Schulman.

leading to his immigration to the United States a dozen years later. But there is a difference between the Romantic Modernism of Frank Lloyd Wright and the Rational Modernism of Richard Neutra.[12] Neutra was in many ways more akin to Le Corbusier in France, and Walter Gropius and Mies Van der Rohe in Germany, whose aim was to unify the machine-made arts and crafts into an architecture that embraced socialist ideals and the forms of the industrial factory. It was only elements from the latter—flat roofs, walls of concrete or glass, and the absence of ornament—that Neutra succeeded in domesticating in southern California, and which in turn exercised a dominant influence upon residential architecture there in the decade before World War II.

A decisive factor in Neutra's immigration to the United States was the earlier departure of his Viennese friend and compatriot, Rudolph Schindler, to work in the Chicago office of Frank Lloyd Wright and, late in 1919, to move to Los Angeles to supervise the construction of the Barnsdall Hollyhock House (1917–1920) from Wright's design. Schindler was settled in southern California when Neutra joined him there in 1925 after working briefly with Wright at Taliesin and with Holabird and Roche in Chicago. Neutra and Schindler entered into an informal partnership which terminated acrimoniously in 1927 when the former was awarded the Lovell Hollywood commission. Schindler had already designed three houses for Phillip Lovell, including the celebrated Newport Beach House (1926), and believed that Neutra had unfairly obtained for himself a significant commission from a long-standing client. What remains historically important from their association is that these two former Viennese architects together created in the Lovell Newport Beach and Hollywood houses "without question . . . the greatest monuments of the early International Style Modern in Southern California."[13] Despite the equality implicit in this critical acclaim, the fortunes of the two architects took radically different turns. Schindler slipped into relative obscurity, while Neutra emerged as California's preeminent practitioner of European Modernism and the first western architect to make the cover of *Time* magazine. This attests not only to Neutra's own architectural corpus—which included prolific writing as well as public, commercial, and residential structures—but also to the authority he exercised over a substantial group of younger designers who were trained in his office.

Some of Neutra's apprentices, like the European-born Raphael Soriano, were content generally to replicate their mentor's flat roofs, ribbon windows, and built-in furniture. But others, such as Gregory Ain and Harwell Hamilton Harris, combined their instruction in Neutra's office with their own approach to design as well as with the ideas of other powerful California architects. Gregory Ain, who, though born in the East, came to Los Angeles as a child and studied architecture at the University of Southern California, worked briefly with Schindler and four years with Neutra. Ain's best-known commission and personal favorite, the Dunsmuir Apartments (1937) in the Baldwin Hills section of Los Angeles, is an exercise in architectural ambivalence. The apartment's street facade is classic Neutra; the garden front celebrates the earlier southern California tradition of Irving Gill with friendly windows, decks and pergolas. In his own writing, Neutra expressed admiration for the work of Gill as an indigenous expression of Modernism. Harwell Hamilton Harris, perhaps the most accomplished of what critics call the Second Generation, is also the most divergent. A native Californian and the son of an architect, Harris's three-year apprenticeship with Neutra is strikingly evident in the Pacific Palisades house he designed in 1937 for John Entenza, later editor of the regional *Arts and Architecture*. But as befitted one who came to architecture by way of sculpture, Harris's later work, such as the influential Havens House designed in 1941 for a steep hillside in Berkeley, shows an affinity with the enduring California wood tradition.

Both Neutra and Wurster, and their followers, left their deepest imprint in the field of residential design. This conformed to another California tradition that whatever had been architecturally most innovative had been achieved in the design of private houses rather than in communal or public buildings. And despite the portentous demographic changes first perceived in the early 1950s, the dominance of the private house as the standard for architectural progression continued for another decade, particularly under the masterful synthesis of Cliff May.

26. Magic-Money House, 1953. Cliff May, architect. Courtesy of the Architectural Drawing Collection, University Art Museum, Santa Barbara.

VII

The Importance of Place

The early work of Richard Neutra and William Wilson Wurster represents a golden age for California and its architecture. In the late 1920s, California had a population under five million and a tolerable balance existed between the people and the land. By 1950, however, the population had more than doubled and the ominous consequences of uncontrolled growth were already perceptible in air pollution, water shortage, devastation of the coastal areas, and wholesale conversion of agricultural land to housing, freeways, and shopping centers. Twenty years later, the population had again doubled to twenty million and California had overtaken New York to become the most populous state in the Union. Economic gains followed demographic ones and California, as the world's sixth ranked economy, constituted a "Nation within a Nation." These swift and dramatic changes grew out of the exigencies of World War II which established the state as the center of nation's shipbuilding and aircraft industries as well as the staging area for fighting the vast Pacific war. The stupendous productivity mobilized in California during the period of World War II did not end with the cessation of hostilities. It continued in the aftermath of warfare as the basis for unprecedented industry and trade and constituted the magnet that attracted to the state a vast population.

The immediate building problem was how to create an architectural vernacular that could provide the millions who were streaming into the state with single-family houses on private lots in conformity to the still prevailing American Dream house. The solution was the "tract house," and among those who most successfully met this design challenge was Cliff May. By linking elements from the turn-of-the-century bungalow and discrete modernisms, May connected his own synthesis of Anglo-Hispanic architecture with Wurster's more refined one to form the California Ranch House that played a dominant role in the development of tract suburbia throughout the United States during the postwar years (Plates 26 and 27).

Cliff May had no formal architectural training, and before entering the housing market, he was a musician, designer, and builder of furniture. But like Wurster, thirteen years his senior, May grew up in California ranching country, spending a part of his boyhood on the Rancho Santa Margarita y Las Flores in San Diego County. On this property, now the United States Marine Corps' Camp Pendleton, was a large Monterey Style adobe with double veranda and patio built after 1864 by Marcos Forster as his home and ranch headquarters. Such early influences are conjectural but could have contributed to May's subsequent career as the nation's leading designer of low cost "western ranch houses." The first of these was the G.I. Ranch House designed for *Good Housekeeping* in 1946, which proved so popular that 70,000 sketch plans were sold within the next decade. *House Beautiful* followed a year later with May's Pace-Setter house for "all pocketbooks, all climates." Also at this time, an important collaboration began with *Sunset* magazine that resulted, among other things, in a number of editions of *Sunset Western Ranch Houses.* This publication introduced May's larger and more expensive designs as well as a dozen examples by Wurster, including the Gregory Farmhouse. Finally in 1950, *Better Homes and Gardens* selected May's "Ranch House for a City Lot" as one of its Five Star Home plans and, after it was constructed at the Chicago World's Fair of that year, it became a national favorite. May produced a pre-cut, packaged synthesis of some of his most popular designs in a series he called Magic-Money Houses and Cliff May Houses (Plates 26 and 27), which by the mid 1950s were not only the most approved tract houses in California but all over America.[1]

Structurally, the Cliff May tract ranch house relied upon simple post and beam construction with economies achieved by prefabricated external and internal wall units, doors, windows, cabinets, and other component parts, crushed-rock roofing instead of shingles, and a concrete slab foundation. Completion of the house was guaranteed in thirty days. The continually up-dated design was pleasing in its neat regularity, conscious contrast between board-and-batten wall surfaces and the large areas of glass doors and windows, and the orientation of the dwelling to an adjacent patio. The houses—light, airy, comfortable, and for their size, spa-

27. Cliff May Houses, Costa Mesa, 1954. Courtesy of the Architectural Drawing Collection, University Art Museum, Santa Barbara.

cious—easily satisfied the criteria Lewis Mumford ascribed to the Wurster proto-type: "good sense and the California wood tradition."[2]

Although advanced Yankee building technology had assured the precedence of wood over adobe construction a hundred years earlier, other elements of Hispanic planning continued to be employed and were essential to the distinctive Ranch House developed by William Wilson Wurster and the later model transformed into a mass medium by Cliff May. Their varying concepts of the Ranch House, combining ingredients common to both the Mediterranean and North American building traditions, fulfilled the Californians's search for an architectural identity to an extent unrealized by the other previous revivals.

Despite the popularity of the California Ranch House, a sustained and important attempt was made in the late 1940s and through the 1950s to challenge its general acceptance as the state's single-family house vernacular. The initiator of this effort was John Entenza, publisher of *Arts & Architecture,* who sought to convince his readers that regionally interpreted modern architecture was equally pleasing and appropriate, and when standardized in production, was economical to build and easy to maintain. To dramatize his convictions, Entenza commissioned the construction of some twenty Case Study Houses in the Los Angeles area. The first, from a design by Neutra for a site in Pacific Palisades, was constructed of plaster and redwood sidings on a wood frame. It was hoped to demonstrate, by the use of traditional methods of construction, regional materials, and carefully planned landscaping, that the severe European "Machine for Living" could be transformed in California into a "Machine in the Garden," whose appeal would reach beyond the usual avant garde modernist clientele. More than half a million people visited the first dozen Case Study Houses in the years between 1945 and 1950. Yet the effort failed; only one of the houses achieved the programmatic objective of acceptance as a prototype for large-scale development. The mass housing market remained firmly committed to the Ranch vernacular. By 1960 the question was moot. The rising costs of land, material, and labor made the custom-built small family house no longer economically viable.

Although the Modernists failed to induce a statewide domestic architectural vernacular, their triumph in the commercial building field was assured when California followed the national conversion to the Corporate International Style. The roots of this stylistic movement were laid in the United States in the late 1930s when Walter Gropius and his successor at the Bauhaus in Germany, Mies van der Rohe, immigrated to America and accepted teaching posts at Harvard University and the Illinois Institute of Technology. Their ideas, however, were not widely accepted until after World War II, when an unprecedented field was created by the explosion of mass building, mass communication, and mass culture. With burgeoning government, education, and corporate institutions waiting for the building design most forcefully expressive of their aspirations, Mies provided a skillful formula readily defined by a modulated, glass-curtain wall that hangs seemingly independent of its structural skeleton. The first American example is Lever House in New York City (1952–1953) by the international firm of Skidmore, Owings and Merrill.

The influence of this building was immense, and six years later the designers of Lever House, with their regional collaborators Hertzka and Knowles, gave California one of its earliest and most representative examples of the eastern prototype in the Crown Zellerbach Building (Plate 28) in San Francisco. The Zellerbach Building is sited only a few blocks from the Hallidie Building (Plate 19), long claimed by Californians to be "the World's First Glass Front Building." The almost half century of time between the construction of these buildings spans a period of enormous change. The wit, intimacy, and originality of Willis Polk's structure cannot be found in the blue-green glass and aluminum tower whose cold anonymity is enforced through the role of imitation. The Zellerbach Building is a faithful expression in California of the "Corporate" style that virtually ruled American commercial construction in the 1960s and 1970s through the national acceptance of the eastern model.

In the northern counties the Lever House-Zellerbach prototype was generally adhered to; in the southern ones the Miesian high rise rectangle was often tilted to the horizontal to produce a more personal and adventuresome architecture. Among the most accomplished practitioners of the Corporate Style in southern California were two architects who came west in the second great immigration following World War II: the Texan, Craig Ellwood, who designed the first of his Case Study Houses in 1952 while still an extension student at UCLA, and the Argentinean Cesar Pelli, who was associated with Eero Saarinen in New York before coming to Los Angeles in 1964. The more orthodox Ellwood designed the Carson Roberts Building in West Hollywood (1960) with a long facade of glass panels above a garage at ground level, thus achieving the "floating" formula admired by the Corporate Stylists. Among the memorable buildings Cesar Pelli produced in California before returning East in 1977 to head the Yale School of Architecture, are the San Bernardino City Hall (1972), with "sculpted" curtain

28. Crown Zellerbach Building, San Francisco, 1959. Skidmore, Owins, and Merrill and Hertzka and Knowles, architects. Courtesy of the Foundation for San Francisco's Architectural Hertage.

walls of alternating opaque spandrels and tinted-glass windows heralding Post-Modernism, and the Pacific Design Center in West Hollywood (1975), whose dark blue glass skin reflects the surrounding cityscape and dramatizes the increasing importance given to place in contemporary California building.

However good as individual examples of design, the endless replication of single or clustered rigid machine-precisioned rectangles provoked a stylistic reaction designated in architectural nomenclatures as Brutalism or New Brutalism. This derivative of the International Style was introduced into California in the 1960s. As Wurster Hall (Plate 29) strikingly reveals, in its varigated and earth-bound monumentality and use of more traditional materials, Brutalism was a response to the increasing banality of the curtain-wall structure. Rough-cast reinforced concrete substituted for precision-machined steel and aluminum; deeply shadowed, irregular openings replaced the endless repetition of thin-revealed windows which usually were sealed in order to lighten the structural load. In contrast to the Miesian glass-walled buildings, Brutalist constructions are inward-oriented, and, as with Wurster Hall, interior plumbing, electrical conduits, and other service equipment are occasionally left exposed.

Brutalism has also been interpreted as a reaction to the anonymity and slickness that came to be associated with corporate bureaucracies operating from buildings patterned on the Miesian formula. Wurster Hall, for example, was inspired in part by Le Corbusier's famous Marseilles housing block, Unite d'Habitation (1946–1952), and conveys the admiration of its architects for this pioneering hero of "Modernism." Their indebtedness is significant because the Unite d'Habitation forcibly reveals the historical and sociological links between the International Style and the nineteenth-century movements that influenced it. These links reappear decisively in the Brutalists's style, particularly as it evolved in the work of Louis I. Kahn and the American-born architects, and point the way to Post-Modernism with its stress upon individuality, history, and the particularity of place.

The inclusion of the factors of history and place within a structure's design has distinguished much of California's recent building from the anonymity of the International Style of the late 1950s and 1960s. Californians, perhaps because of the relative brevity of their own recorded history, have long demanded that architecture convey historical import—hence the succession of regional revivals from Mission through Spanish Colonial to California Ranch House. This contributed to a regional acceptance of the Brutalist phase of the Modernist Movement

29. Wurster Hall, Berkeley, 1964. Esherick, Homsey, Dodge and Davis and Vernon DeMars and Donald Olsen, architects. Photograph by Rondal Partridge. Courtesy of the architects.

no longer so readily accorded to the earlier Miesian corporate prototype. An exciting example of how a building design can relate both to history and environment is the Salk Institute of Biological Studies (Plate 30), completed at La Jolla in 1965. The design clearly falls into the category of Brutalism, but architect Louis I. Kahn endowed the reinforced concrete structure with a sense of space, humanism, and ceremony that relates directly to the Beaux-Arts tradition that has been dominant in California since Albert Pissis's Hibernia Bank of 1892 (Plate 18). The rediscovery of history in architecture is one of the main tenets of Post-Modernism and a worldwide phenomenon. One of its leading Italian theorists proclaimed the movement's purpose as the return of architecture "to the womb of history, and its recycling in new syntactic contents of traditional forms."[3] The intent of Post-Modernism was succinctly stated in the slogan of the 1980 Venice Biennale: "The Presence of the Past."

The presence of the past is a constant theme in California architecture; the precepts of Vitruvius and Palladio have defined topical building in many of its phases from the Franciscans to the Post-Modernists. Among the latter, Charles W. Moore's California commissions show how a powerful syntax can emerge from the re-use of traditional forms. Moore's fusion of regional elements within their territory is brilliantly exemplified in his work at Sea Ranch on the isolated Mendocino coast more than a hundred miles north of San Francisco (Plate 31). The site of this ongoing project mirrors the northern California coast much as it was first seen by the immigrants of 1849 after the shout "Gold" was heard around the world. The isolated splendor of the Sea Ranch's site, five thousand acres of meadows and wooded hills, acts as a restricting force upon the several hundred buildings that have been constructed there. Landscape architects Lawrence Halprin and Associates sought to organize the building sites in clusters surrounded by open spaces or commons and advocated the propagation of native plants in their natural setting. The architectural program prescribed that the design of the houses, condominiums, stores, restaurants, and a motel conform to the environment, including its regional history. In accordance with this specification, the buildings designed by Moore and his associates reflect such historic neighboring types as the weathered remnants of Fort Ross, constructed in the early nineteenth century from the memory of the Russian colony at Sitka, and the traditional frame houses and barns of the New England settlers of the 1850s and 1860s. The latter structures, and particularly their angled and shed roofs, furnish the chief source of what has become virtually a Sea Ranch style. The result is that the old forms,

30. The Salk Institute, La Jolla, 1959–1965. Louis I. Kahn, architect. Courtesy of the Salk Institute.

superimposed upon a new land almost a century and a half earlier, have themselves become the presence of the past to new generations of Californians.

Although born and bred a midwesterner, Charles Moore acquired by way of youthful winters spent in Pasadena an early affinity with California. This attraction was nourished through the practice and teaching of architecture in the Bay Area in the 1960s and in Los Angeles in the next two decades. His work and influence, which has been considerable in both the northern and southern parts of the state, manifest a consistent aversion to Modernism. Moore always scorned "the Cartesian Abstractions" of the Internationalists, favoring instead the historical and emotional elements which lay outside of the Modernists' vocabulary. "Traditions," Moore insisted, "have great power precisely because they present us with possibilities and guides that can support invention."[4] Rejecting the purism of the Miesians, Moore celebrates the paradoxical and the complex; for him, more is not less. Along with his wit and historicism, he gives to Californians an enlarged "sense of place." In his earlier work, especially at Sea Ranch, the dominant influences suggest the New England heritage and the Shingle Style. The southern California commissions of the 1970s look back to the whole range of western architecture as well as the regionally shared Hispanic past.

The varied forms through which architects trained in the established traditions of Europe and the eastern United States adapted to the topical demands of the San Francisco and Los Angeles areas largely constitutes the history of California's building. Reflecting upon the fact that "Maybeck, Polk, Schweinfurt and Coxhead all came here from entirely different environments," Joseph Esherick, one of Charles Moore's colleagues in the creation of Sea Ranch, concluded that it was the same for himself: "I don't come from here, so I had to figure it out."[5] The youthful Esherick, who arrived in San Francisco in 1938 from the northeastern United States with an architectural degree from the University of Pennsylvania as well as training in sculpture and woodworking, updates the professional profile of the American-born immigrant architect that has pertained since the Gold Rush. Esherick began his California career in the office of Gardiner Daily, who after William Wilson Wurster was the leader in what Lewis Mumford came to label the Bay Region Style and defined as "a native and humane form of Modernism."[6] Esherick's mastery of the regional mystique was first evident in a series of summer houses at Lake Tahoe in the late 1940s, which revealed the architect's unusual sensitivity to place as well as to the work of his Shingle Style predecessors. In 1952, he began a thirty-year teaching stint at the Berkeley School of Architecture

31. Condominium I, Sea Ranch, 1965. Moore, Lyndon, Turnbull and Whitaker, architects. Photograph by David Gebhard.

of the University of California, where among his students were George Homsey, Peter Dodge, and Charles Davis. These three joined their mentor in 1963 to form the continuing partnership that five years later received the Architectural Firm Award of the American Institute of Architects. One of only four California offices ever to be so distinguished, the firm's design for the Hermitage (Plate 32) is exemplary for the way the elements of history and place can be integrated into a building to satisfy fully the demands of its environment.

The Hermitage is a condominium structure on San Francisco's Russian Hill, an area of considerable historical and architectural importance. Russian Hill was initially the burial place for sea otter and seal hunters from the Sitka colony in Alaska; later it became the haunt of San Francisco's *fin de siècle* writers and artists; presently it is one of the city's most distinguished residential neighborhoods. The site proposed for the Hermitage was a particularly sensitive one, for despite being architecturally among the most richly endowed areas in California, it was for years the battleground between preservationist-minded neighbors and developers, who planned to construct a twenty-two story apartment complex. When the high-rise proposal finally was rejected, one of the neighbors purchased the site and commissioned Esherick, Homsey, Dodge, and Davis to design a building compatible with the immediate surroundings. These included several steeply gabled houses from the 1880s by a masterful if unknown hand; more than half a dozen dwellings by Willis Polk, including the house he built for himself in 1892; and directly fronting the site, one of the finest survivors of Julia Morgan's extensive domestic work. That the Hermitage would be defined by unpainted shingles, gable roofs, and bay windows was accepted by the architects as a historical necessity. However, for the building's major decorative motifs, they turned to the concrete balustrades and retaining walls created by Willis Polk for this and other San Francisco hills which first appeared as part of Daniel Burnham's great plan for the city in 1904.

In designing the Monterey Bay Aquarium (Plate 33), situated not far from the Larkin House (Plate 4) and built upon one of the factories celebrated in John Steinbeck's *Cannery Row,* Esherick, Homsey, Dodge, and Davis presented another example of how a building scheme can honor both its territory and its usage. The aquarium was designed in part from lessons the firm learned earlier in its recycling of an old cannery at San Francisco's Fisherman's Wharf into a multilevel center of shops and restaurants. The keystone of the Monterey Bay Aquarium project was the preservation of the historical surroundings as embodied

32. The Hermitage, San Francisco, 1982. Esherick, Homsey, Dodge and Davis, architects. Photograph by Peter Aaron. Courtesy of the architects.

33. Monterey Bay Aquarium, Monterey, 1984. Esherick, Homsey, Dodge and Davis, architects. Photograph by Jane Lidz. Courtesy of the architects.

in the canning factory shown in the extreme right of Plate 33, and the integration of the region's rich marine environment and sea-life with a modern exhibition hall that would accommodate great numbers of people in an atmosphere both educative and friendly. The historical objective was achieved by integrating the pump house boilers of the older building into the design of the new structure and then reconstructing the original smokestacks. The aquarium's style thus derived logically from the proportions, roof pitches, and building materials of the American industrial tradition of the 1920s and 1930s. In their efforts to bring the aquarium structure into harmony with the physical environment, the architects consulted old Cannery Row workers and residents, the California Coastal Commission, and field and marine biologists. The resulting transition from natural to enclosed marine space has been praised as establishing within the aquarium the same sense of "order, grandeur, and harmony" as exists in the waters that surround it.[7]

The style of the Monterey Aquarium is High-Tech, one of the many manifestations of Post-Modernism. Its roots lie both in the machine and the factory and in the architectonic order revealed in industrial photography and precisionist painting of the second quarter of the present century. From the latter, particularly the paintings of Charles Sheeler, come the sharp edges, clearly defined planes, and brilliant Cubist-inspired colors. More immediately, the style is rooted in the work of the minimal sculptors of the 1960s, whose stress upon the concept of art as process is firmly shared by Frank Gehry, one of the California masters of High-Tech design. Frank Gehry, like almost all the state's other influential architects, followed the paths of immigrants to California. Arriving in Los Angeles from Canada in 1947 at the age of eighteen, he worked his way through the University of Southern California School of Architecture with an apprenticeship in the office of Victor Gruen Associates, and completed his professional education at the Harvard School of Design. Here the Modernist influence of Walter Gropius was balanced by that of Joseph Hudnut, who led him to the study of architectural history. In this pursuit, Gehry spent a year in Europe where he was especially drawn to Romanesque building and the seventeenth-century churches of Francesco Borromini. Gehry carried back this memory of Europe's past with him to southern California in 1962, where he established a practice that to date has found its most eloquent and creative statement in the Loyola Law School (Plate 34).

The Loyola Law School program called for faculty offices, classrooms, lecture halls, a student center, and a chapel, all within a confined and somewhat hostile

34. Loyola Law School. Los Angeles, 1981–1984. Frank Gehry, architect. Photograph by Michael Moran. Courtesy of Michael Moran.

part of downtown Los Angeles. The human problem was how to endow a dis-spirited faculty and student body with a sense of place and pride that would encourage them to remain on campus between classes and participate in extra-curricular discussion and activity. In meeting this challenge, Gehry resisted the usual urban solution of combining the multipurpose facilities within a single massive structure. Instead, he turned to Thomas Jefferson's plan for the University of Virginia and created "an academical village"; a place, as Gehry expressed it after meeting with faculty and students, "that provides, as you walk from class to class, the feeling that you're in an environment of the law."[8] Also, as was the case with Jefferson, Gehry's model was Rome. But the concept of Rome he projected through time and space to California included the Baroque city of Borromini as well as the ancient forums. The plan centers upon a large rectangular building painted a rich ochre color and topped by a glass temple symbolizing the light of scholarship. This main building separates the campus-forum from the street and serves as a backdrop for the three small lecture halls and chapel whose designs suggest, but do not imitate, classical forms. Gehry enlivened Republican Roman severity with Baroque movement by placing the main building's stairways across the vertical axis of the exterior facade to create the image of a soaring fountain falling into cascades. The overall effect is a sense of animation and interest that transforms an otherwise constricted urban environment into a charming and intimate space inviting leisure and reflection. The Loyola Law School also fulfills beautifully its designer's intent to testify to a confused and rootless time and place the historical Western traditions shared both by architecture and law.

The plywood and glass construction of the tiny Loyola Law School chapel suggests the "unfinished" nature of Gehry's art as well as the condition of the California profession at large. Although Gehry's preference for the unfinished is said to come from painting and sculpture, it derives logically from the history and rhythm of his adopted state, and especially its major city. The in-process quality of life, characterized chiefly as movement, is nowhere more evident than in Los Angeles, where a society and its architecture flourish with little discernible direction or guidance. In times so unstable and fragmented, is it not reasonable, Gehry asks of his profession, to learn from all who can teach? This question is particularly meaningful today when the Modern Movement is seen as but another phase in a long history of styles and not, as its ideologues fervently preached, the consumation of architectural experience and expression. Thus freed from prescriptive rules, and yet still open to Old World and eastern American influences,

Californians are creating an architecture that eschews stylistic definition for immediacy, fantasy, surprise, and wit. The form it takes will be shaped by the state's now several hundred years old architectural tradition, the spaciousness and diversity of the land, the continuing cycles of immigration, and an adventurous and still youthful profession.

Notes

Chapter One

1. The late eighteenth-century descriptions by Miguel Costansó, Juan Crespí, and Pédro Fages are given in Edith Buckland Webb, *Indian Life at the Old Missions* (Los Angeles: Warren F. Lewis, 1952), 9, 13-14; and Pedro Fages, *A Historical, Political and Natural Description of California,* trans. Herbert I. Priestly (Berkeley and Los Angeles: University of California Press, 1937), 48.

2. See the drawings made in 1850 of Yurok structures in Georgia Willis Read and Ruth Gains, eds., *Gold Rush: The Journals, Drawings, and Other Papers of J. Goldsborough Bruff* (New York: Columbia University Press, 1944), I: 410–412. The general authenticity of the Mattz House is verified in Alfred L. Kroeber, *Handbook of the Indians of California* (Washington, D.C.: Smithsonian Institution, 1925), plates 9–14.

3. Robert Heizer and M. A. Whipple, eds., *The California Indians: A Source Book* (Berkeley and Los Angeles: University of California Press, 1971), 8–9, 337–338.

Chapter Two

1. Webb, *Indian Life,* 8.

2. Richard Henry Dana, *Two Years Before the Mast* (1840; reprint, New York: Harper and Row, 1965), 65.

Chapter Three

1. David Gebhard explores the possibility that the Alpheus P. Thompson Adobe in Santa Barbara predates the Larkin House by several months in "Some Additional Observations

on California's Monterey Tradition," *Journal of the Society of Architectural Historians* XLVI (1987): 162.

2. Robert J. Parker, "Building the Larkin House," *California Historical Society Quarterly* XVI (1937): 321–335.

3. Joseph Warren Revere, *Naval Duty in California* (Oakland: Biobooks, 1947), 146.

4. Hubert Howe Bancroft, *California Pioneer Register and Index, 1542–1848* (Baltimore: Regional Publishing Co., 1964), 114.

Chapter Four

1. Ralph Waldo Emerson, *Journals* (Boston: Houghton Mifflin, 1912), 8: 1.

2. Frank Marryat, *Mountains and Molehills* (New York: Harper & Brothers, 1855), 38.

3. See Plates 19, 27, 35, and 36 in Harold Kirker, *California's Architectural Frontier* (San Marino: The Huntington Library, 1960).

4. *Ibid.,* 52.

5. Newton Arvin, ed., *The Selected Letters of Henry Adams* (New York: Farrar, Straus and Young, 1951), 247.

6. Zoeth Skinner Eldredge, *History of California* (New York: Century History Company, 1915), 5: 472.

7. Agnes Foster Buchanan, "Some Early Business Buildings of San Francisco," *Architectural Record,* XX (1906): 15.

8. Pictured in the seven-plate daguerreotype panorama of 1851 that is owned by the California Historical Society. William Ingraham Kip, *The Early Days of My Episcopate* (New York: Thomas Whittaker, 1892), 71.

9. Illustrated in V. Aubrey Neasham, *The City of the Plain* (Sacramento: Sacramento Pioneer Foundation, 1969), 76.

10. Benjamin E. Lloyd, *Lights and Shades in San Francisco* (San Francisco: A. L. Bancroft, 1876), 273.

Chapter Five

1. Joseph Cather Newsom, *Picturesque and Artistic Homes and Buildings of California* (San Francisco, 1890), 24.

2. Richard Longstreth to the author, Manhattan, Kansas, 18 August 1982.

3. Karen J. Weitze, *California's Mission Revival* (Los Angeles: Hennessey and Ingalls, 1984), 21–22.

4. Weitze, *California's Mission Revival,* 21.

5. *Ibid.,* 21.

6. Felix Rey, "A Tribute to Mission Style," *Architect and Engineer,* LXXIX (1924): 78.

7. Franklin Dickerson Walker, *A Literary History of Southern California* (Berkeley and Los Angeles: University of California Press, 1950), 132.

8. Weitze, *California's Mission Revival,* 16.

9. Esther McCoy, *Five California Architects* (New York: Reinhold Publishing Corporation, 1960), 61.

Chapter Six

1. For the material on Albert Pissis and Arthur Brown, Jr., I am indebted to the research of Dr. Christopher Nelson.

2. Henry Hope Reed, *The Golden City* (New York: W. W. Norton, 1971), 93.

3. David Gebhard, et al., *A Guide to Architecture in San Francisco and Northern California* (Santa Barbara and Salt Lake City: Peregrine Smith, Inc., 1973), 81.

4. Bernard R. Maybeck, *Palace of Fine Arts and Lagoon* (San Francisco: Paul Elder and Company, 1915), 9–10.

5. Charles Moore, Peter Becker, and Regula Campbell, *The City Observed: Los Angeles* (New York: Random House, 1984), 84.

6. *Ibid.,* 184.

7. Quoted in *Architectural Record,* CXIX (1956): 222.

8. William Wilson Wurster, "California Architecture for Living," *California Monthly,* XLIV (April 1954): 14, 16.

9. Citation accompanying the American Institute of Architects' Gold Medal, presented June 26, 1969, bound with the William Wilson Wurster oral history interview, conducted by Suzanne B. Riess in Berkeley in 1964 for the University of California Library Regional Cultural History Project, Bancroft Library.

10. *Ibid.,* 101.

11. Reyner Banham, *Los Angeles: The Architecture of Four Ecologies* (New York: Harper & Row, 1971), 189.

12. See Thomas S. Hines, "Rationalism and Reintegration, 1920–1980," *Los Angeles Transfer: Architecture in Southern California, 1880–1980* (Los Angeles: University of California, William Andrews Clark Memorial Library, 1983), 59.

13. David Gebhard and Robert Winter, *Architecture in Los Angeles* (Salt Lake City: Gibbs Smith, Inc., 1985), 179.

Chapter 7

1. For the material on Cliff May, I am indebted to the research of David Bricker.

2. Wurster oral history, 270.

3. Paolo Portoghesi, *Postmodern: The Architecture of the Postindustrial World* (New York: Rizzoli, 1983), 14.

4. Charles Moore, Gerald Allen, and Donlyn Lyndon, *The Place of House* (New York: Holt, Rinehart and Winston, 1974), vii.

5. *Architecture California,* VIII (1986), 23.

6. Lewis Mumford, "The Skyline," *New Yorker Magazine,* XXIII (1947): 99.

7. Thomas Hoving, "Museum of the Sea," *Connoisseur,* CCXV (1985): 89.

8. Peter Arnell and Ted Bickford, *Frank Gehry: Buildings and Projects* (New York: Rizzoli, 1985), XVII.

Bibliography

The study of architecture begins with the object, and preferably the object *in situ*. This imperative has governed my methodology: a series of specific extant structures employed to illustrate the story of California architecture from prehistory to the present. The only exceptions are the two representative examples of San Francisco's long-vanished Gold Rush buildings. The standard guides to California's extant architecture are David Gebhard, Robert Winter, et al., *Architecture in San Francisco & Northern California* and *Architecture in Los Angeles & Southern California* (Santa Barbara and Salt Lake City: Peregrine Smith, Inc., 1973, 1977). Sally B. Woodbridge, *California Architecture* (San Francisco: Chronicle Books, 1988), contains more than one thousand entries from the Historic American Buildings Survey; G. E. Kidder Smith, *The Architecture of the United States: The Plains and Far West* (Garden City, New York: Anchor Books, 1981), includes seventy-seven California subjects. Supplementing these statewide studies is a growing body of local guides, such as John Chase, *The Sidewalk Companion to Santa Cruz Architecture* (Santa Cruz: Paper Vision Press, 1979); Robert Bruegmann, *Benicia: Portrait of an Early California Town* (San Francisco: 101 Productions, 1980); Dorothy F. Regnery, *An Enduring Heritage: Historic Buildings of the San Francisco Peninsula* (Stanford: Stanford University Press, 1976); and Rebecca Conard and Christopher Nelson, *Santa Barbara: A Guide to El Pueblo Viejo* (Santa Barbara: Capra Press, 1986). The indispensable overview of California architecture *in situ* is Mildred Brooke Hoover, Hero Eugene Rensch, and Ethel Grace Rensch, *Historic Spots in California* (Stanford: Stanford University Press, 1970).

The single general history of the state's architecture—mainly covering the nineteenth century—is my *California's Architectural Frontier* (San Marino: Huntington Library, 1960 and Santa Barbara and Salt Lake City: Peregrine Smith, Inc., 1973 and 1986). In the quarter-century since its publication, there has been an increasing number of monographic works beginning with Esther McCoy, *Five California Architects* (New York: Reinhold, 1960), four of whose subjects subsequently have received separate treatment: Randell L. Makinson, *Greene and Greene* (Salt Lake City: Peregrine Smith, Inc., 1977); Kenneth Cardwell, *Bernard Maybeck* (Salt Lake City, Peregrine Smith, Inc., 1977); and David Gebhard, *Schindler* (New York: Viking Press, 1972). For Schindler's Viennese compatriot, see Thomas S. Hines, *Richard Neutra and the Search for Modern Architecture* (New York: Oxford University Press, 1982). Ernest Coxhead and Willis Polk are the central subjects of Richard Longstreth, *On the Edge of the World* (Cambridge: MIT Press, 1983). California's most celebrated woman architect is eulogized in Sara Holmes Boutelle, *Julia Morgan, Architect* (New York: Abbeville Press, 1988).

Both San Francisco and Los Angeles have induced a distinguished architectural literature. For the northern city this includes the Historic Site Project of the Junior League, *Here Today* (San Francisco: Chronicle Books, 1968); the Foundation for San Francisco's Architectural Heritage, *Splendid Survivors* (San Francisco: California Living Books, 1979); Ruth Hendricks Willard and Carol Green Wilson, *Sacred Places* (San Francisco: Presidio Press, 1985); Robert C. Bernhardi, *Great Buildings of San Francisco* (New York: Dover Publications, Inc., 1980); and Sally Woodbridge, ed., *Bay Area Houses* (New York: Oxford University Press, 1976). Los Angeles's architectural history has been advanced by Reyner Banham, *Los Angeles: The Architecture of Four Ecologies* (New York: Harper and Row, 1971); Paul Gleye, *The Architecture of Los Angeles* (Los Angeles: Rosebud Books, 1981); Charles C. Moore, Peter Becker, and Regula Campbell, *The City Observed* (New York: Random House, 1984); David Gebhard and Robert Winter, *Architecture in Los Angeles* (Salt Lake City: Gibbs Smith, Inc., 1985); and Sam Hall Kaplan, *LA: Lost & Found* (New York: Crown Publications, Inc., 1987), the latter a treasury of architectural photography largely by Julius Shulman.

As yet little has been written regarding California's participation in the architectural revivals of the nineteenth and early twentieth centuries. A notable exception is Karen Weitze, *The Mission Revival* (Los Angeles: Hennessey & Ingalls, 1985). David Gebhard has written authoritatively on the Spanish Colonial Revival, particularly *Santa Barbara: The Creation of a New Spain in America* (Santa Barbara: University Art Museum, 1982). The domestication of the Richardsonian Romanesque in California is treated in Paul V. Turner, *The Founders & the Architects: The Design of Stanford University* (Stanford: Department of Art, 1976). Of related interest is Robert Winter, *The California Bungalow* (Los Angeles: Hennessey & Ingalls, 1980).

There is a body of periodical literature that began in 1880 with the publication of the monthly *California Architect and Building News*. It was superseded in 1900 by *The Architect and Engineer of California,* which continued until 1959. The *Journal of the Society of Architectural Historians* has occasionally published scholarly research on California, such as Elisabeth Kendall Thompson, "The Early Domestic Architecture of the San Francisco Bay Region," X (Oct. 1951); Keith W. Dills, "The Hallidie Building," XXX (Dec. 1971); and Reyner Banham, "The Plot Against Bernard Maybeck," XLIII (Mar. 1984). Significant architectural studies from the California Historical Society *Quarterly* (since 1971 *California History*) are Robert J. Parker, "Building the Larkin House," XVI (Dec. 1937); and Anne Bloomfield, "David Farquharson: Pioneer California Architect," LIX (Spring 1980). This material is augmented by periodic publications of a growing number of regional historical and preservation societies.

Index